D1423439

Praise for *Service Intelligence*

"Sharon Taylor has earned the respect of the service management industry for her willingness to stretch the boundaries of conventional wisdom, for example, by extending the principles of service management through to the full service lifecycle."

—Ian Head, Research Director, Service Management and Process Improvement, Gartner Inc.

"This book is a really practical, broad-based, and friendly explanation of why service management is so important for delivering better service faster and at lower cost. It is written by an expert with international status, who has personally shaped the way the service management industry operates.

—Jenny Dugmore, Director of Service Matters and Chair of the ISO/IEC 20000 Series Committee

"Customers, vendors and practitioners can all learn from the experience of Sharon Taylor when it comes to implementing IT Service Management concepts."

—Markos Symeonides, Executive Vice President, Axios Systems

"Best practices in the field of IT Service Management today have matured as a result of Sharon Taylor's commitment to and leadership in the industry. Her contributions while Chairman of itSMF International and work in authoring numerous ITSM books have helped to spread the adoption of IT best practice across the globe. Taylor is one of the most well-respected thought leaders in our industry. It is, therefore, no surprise that she was awarded the ITSM Lifetime Achievement Award in 2008."

—Emily Sturm, Marketing Manager, Axios Systems

"*Service Intelligence* is excellent because it is easy to read, easy to follow, and easy to understand, which for me, are the basic tenets upon which the best business and technical books are built. Full of examples and supporting graphics, the journey through the book progresses without confusion or the need to constantly refer back to earlier chapters. The lessons contained in the book will be invaluable to all organizations, both large and small."

—Malcolm Fry

"Sharon Taylor 'breaks the eye.' She takes familiar context and provides fresh, evaluated views of IT service management at its leading edges. It's a work sure to find its way into practitioners' back pockets."
—Michael Nieves

"Sharon Taylor has succeeded in bringing together all the necessary pieces to teach business leaders how to negotiate, foster, control, and nurture a healthy relationship with their IT service provider. This is a must read for anyone seeking successful ITSM partnerships."
—Pauline Angelico, Managing Director Plus Green IT, MD Itilics, CEO Marval Asia Pacific

"Sharon Taylor's leadership continues to drive adoption and maturity in the service management profession and the abilities of those who practice it."
—Dennis G. Ravenelle, Network Integration Project Manager, Harvard University Information Technology

Service Intelligence

Service Intelligence

Improving Your Bottom Line with the Power of IT Service Management

Sharon Taylor

PRENTICE
HALL

Upper Saddle River, NJ • Boston • Indianapolis • San Francisco
New York • Toronto • Montreal • London • Munich • Paris • Madrid
Cape Town • Sydney • Tokyo • Singapore • Mexico City

The publisher offers excellent discounts on this book when ordered in quantity for bulk purchases or special sales, which may include electronic versions and/or custom covers and content particular to your business, training goals, marketing focus, and branding interests. For more information, please contact:

U.S. Corporate and Government Sales
(800) 382-3419
corpsales@pearsontechgroup.com

For sales outside the United States, please contact:

International Sales
international@pearson.com

Visit us on the Web: informit.com/ph

The Library of Congress cataloging-in-publication data is on file.

ISBN-13: 978-0-13-269207-6
ISBN-10: 0-13-269207-4
Text printed in the United States on recycled paper at R.R. Donnelley in Crawfordsville, Indiana.
First printing August 2011

Editor-in-Chief
Greg Wiegand

Senior Acquisitions Editor
Katherine Bull

Development Editor
Candace Dunwoodie

Technical Editor
Ivor Macfarlane

Managing Editor
Kristy Hart

Project Editor
Jovana San Nicolas-Shirley

Copy Editor
Water Crest Publishing, Inc.

Indexer
Lisa Stumpf

Proofreader
Michael Henry

Publishing Coordinator
Cindy Teeters

Cover Designer
Alan Clements

Compositor
Nonie Ratcliff

For all who journey through the challenges of giving, receiving, and recognizing quality service management. For those who provide it through leading by example and energizing their organizations to never settle for less than their best practices.

Contents

Preface

This book is a compilation of the basics of IT Service Management drawn from the leading best practices in the industry. It is presented from a business point of view and is intended to inform, educate, and provoke a new level of thinking by business leaders about the importance and relevance of IT Service Management to their companies.

As with all best practices, time turns them into common practices, and the next innovation in thought leadership will create new best practices. The topics included in this book are intended to stand the test of time and form the basis for strong service partnerships, which will make service excellence commonplace in companies and become the benchmark for others to innovate from.

The IT Service Management industry offers a wealth of information and platforms for the exchange of ideas. Until this book, most of this was written for the ITSM industry and its providers. Now, in these pages, business finds a home within ITSM, and by offering ITSM a place at the corporate table, can reap the benefits of decades of practice by other high-performing businesses.

Acknowledgments

I would like to acknowledge the following individuals, without whom this book could not have achieved its best.

Katherine Bull, Pearson, who believed in the idea of a book about ITSM that would help business achieve more.

Ivor Macfarlane, IBM, a service management pioneer and my mentor from the early days of ITSM and still today for his thorough and thought-provoking technical review.

Candace Dunwoodie, Aspect Group Inc., a highly respected business thought leader who kept all of us real with her sharp style of review and challenging perspective.

Very special thanks to my family, who through their sacrifice of my absence, their patience, motivation, and support made this book achievable and finished on time.

About the Author

Sharon Taylor, President of the Aspect Group, is a well-known and respected figure within today's IT Service Management community.

As the former Chief Architect and current Chief Examiner for ITIL®, the world's leading IT Service Management best practices, she has shaped the direction of ITSM and helped hundreds of companies achieve their service management goals.

Sharon is the author of numerous service management books, is a regular columnist for a variety of global IT management publications, and is a sought-after keynote speaker in the industry.

She was the Chairman of the Board for the Chair of the itSMF International, an IT service management forum responsible for ensuring global growth and governance of ITSMF in more than 50 countries. The itSMF is at the center of best practice development and endorsement.

Sharon is also past President of the North American Institute of Certified Service Management Professionals and the recipient of the prestigious ITSM Lifetime Achievement Award, which is voted on by experts in the IT industry.

Her contributions to the community and to best practice are based upon her extensive professional experience in the industry.

As the President of Aspect Group Inc., she is leading AGI's consultancy, training, and ITSM practice, working with clients throughout North America, Asia, and Europe.

As a long-time CEO, Sharon brings a business background and focus to IT service management and devotes her business experience to influencing the directions of the IT service management industry.

Introduction

Do you ever have days where you come across a concept so simple, yet so powerful, that you wished you'd thought of it yourself? Of course—we all do. Today is one of those days. By picking up this book, you will have started a journey of "a-ha" moments that will leave you wondering why someone didn't tell you this a long time ago. Well, chances are, they have.

Some experts estimate that there are over 3 billion computers in the world. Take a walk around your place of business and count the number of people using PCs, telephones, PDAs, and fax machines.

To have a conversation with another person, you can email, chat, tweet, instant message, RSS, phone, or see them in person (most often occurring in somewhat that order). A meeting can be conducted in a boardroom with colleagues but is more likely today to be done virtually with video, audio, and shared workspaces instantly with people from across the planet.

As a business leader, you know the value technology has brought to your organization and the tremendous competitive advantage, workforce productivity, and overall cost savings you can gain from its use. You also know that when things go wrong, the cost can be staggering.

Technology is so embedded in our culture that we forget that things can and will go wrong at times. Fortunately, seemingly by some mystical force, though, technology for the most part works around the clock to serve our needs.

Just about everything we do depends on technology, is run using technology, or is developed using it.

There is no mystical force at play, however. In order for technology to unlock business potential, it must be managed with vision, direction, and expertise. The pace of competitive business today requires IT management

1

to be somewhat clairvoyant at times. The ability of IT to predict and respond to business need keeps a business competitive and customers loyal.

There is one and only one set of methods in the world that has proven to be resilient and robust enough to enable it to do this: IT Service Management, better known in the IT industry as ITSM.

This book is not about IT. It is about how ITSM can empower your business to achieve better profits. This book is about finding those ITSM "a-ha" moments. It will show you how to make sure you recognize the characteristics of good ITSM and how to make sure you get them from your IT service.

Why Read This Book?

It's Friday at 6:00 p.m. You've just finished a long work week and are rushing to catch the train home. It's a long holiday weekend, and you plan to enjoy it with family and friends. You'll need some cash, so you make a quick stop at the ATM machine before the train arrives.

As you round the corner, you notice that there is no line at your favorite ATM. What luck! The weekend is shaping up wonderfully! As you pluck your bank card from your wallet, you see it from the corner of your eye, glaring back at you: "THIS MACHINE IS TEMPORARILY OUT OF SERVICE." That explains why there is no line. No problem. You'll just get cash at an ATM in the train station.

At the station, you go from one ATM to the next, all of them blasting the dreaded message: "THIS MACHINE IS TEMPORARILY OUT OF SERVICE" (see Figure I-1). How is this possible? By now, you have missed the train and will have to wait 45 more minutes for the next, all because the ATM service was down.

We all have experienced the frustration of services "temporarily" out of order. We think of this as terribly inconvenient and aggravating, but we move on. However, this service disruption, which is an aggravation to us, has far worse consequences for the business.

Three hours earlier, at the bank's ATM data center, a software analyst has just finished amending some application code to the ATM welcome screen. It's been a slow afternoon, so he is pleased to be catching up on some of the minor changes that never seem to get done.

FIGURE I-1   ATM machine

These types of minor code updates don't affect any customer account data, or require an application to be taken offline to restart, so the change is added while the ATM network service remains online. The analyst completes the update, closes the log, and goes for coffee. The analyst does not realize that this update contains errors and the system keeps repeatedly trying to apply the update, which the system cannot accept.

The ATM service is very sophisticated and has built in security monitoring. The system is programmed to automatically shut down the ATM system when a security issue or intrusion attempt is detected. The repeated attempts to apply the code update triggers an alarm with the system's security monitor. The system reacts as though there is a possible security breach and sends a command to shut down all the ATMs. Five minutes later, hundreds of ATM machines are rendered out of service. One of the bank's critical services goes offline just as 3 million people are leaving their offices, looking for money for the holiday weekend.

At the same time, the bank's service desk is noticing an abrupt increase in the number of calls. Reports of ATM service outages are tumbling in like waves on the shoreline.

Not long after, the phone of the bank's Senior Vice President rings. Interrupting her from dinner, she takes the call and learns that the bank's entire ATM service is down. Using her years of experience at the bank, she quickly estimates that this is costing the bank about a million dollars a minute. This is hour four.

Someone will be fired over this for sure. This company has not yet heard of ITSM...unfortunately. Ironically, the reality is that this service failure was easily preventable.

Illuminating Your Vulnerabilities

The previous scenario is a fictitious account of an IT service failure that happens much too often in reality. The use of ITSM could have prevented this from happening in the first place. From an impact perspective, this means ITSM could have saved the business from the following problems:

- Financial losses in the millions for ATM transactions that could not be completed

- Reputation losses for poor customer service

- Bad publicity that harms the bank's image

- Loss of customer loyalty

- Loss of customers

- Opportunity for competitors to take customers away

From a business perspective, ITSM is about managing service quality, reliability, and business performance. Keeping services available, especially when they are most needed, is a prime business need, which, in this case, failed to happen.

ITSM illuminates where business vulnerabilities are and how to address them *before* they create an issue. A key ITSM concept is using processes embedded in the service culture that never take their eyes off the implications to business outcomes and knowing what customers want. In the previous fictitious scenario, there seems in hindsight to be a number of glaring deficiencies in safeguarding the uninterrupted operation of the business critical ATM network service. From an ITSM perspective, this reveals that the Bank's business processes are vulnerable to a lack of control within the IT organization. Had the Bank used ITSM processes embedded for any change to critical services, no matter how seemingly minor, this event would not have occurred. The software analyst in the scenario would have known the criticality of the service and the potential vulnerability that an uncontrolled change would induce.

The scenario also uncovers an additional vulnerability. Not only is there a lack of control around changes, but a gap in IT continuity for offering customers alternative ways to access their funds in the event of a catastrophic failure.

Successful companies all have predictable and consistent characteristics that, in part, define why they are successful. Regardless of the business you are in, attention to quality management is one of these characteristics. Those who fail to pay attention to this ultimately cease to exist. ITSM is to quality management what water is to life. Without it, your business is at costly and totally avoidable risk.

Capitalizing on Your Strengths

ITSM is quality management for IT. It ensures that not only does the technology functions as we need it to, but it also ensures that when the unexpected happens, there are actions ready to be taken to minimize the impact to business. Because of ITSM, we know what our customers want, think, and feel about the service we provide. ITSM helps us recognize and seize opportunities to innovate and improve services as they arise, and not as an afterthought or reaction to an unhappy customer experience.

So, how do you get this kind of ITSM? By understanding what it is (and isn't), how to negotiate with suppliers that offer it, and what it should look like in your company.

ITSM—In Good Company

ITSM has been around for decades. It has turned good companies into excellent ones. It has saved millions of dollars and reputations during this time. This book highlights a few of those poignant moments.

It is used by large, medium, and small companies. ITSM is recognized by international standards organizations and is used worldwide.

ITSM is a set of best practice frameworks, developed over years, to manage IT using positive, measurable, repeatable, and consistent results—sort of like what you would want your balance sheet to do!

These are simple, yet powerful, truths. However, oversimplification can lead to negative consequences, even with ITSM. The most successful companies in the world use ITSM, and they know that the best way to exploit the power of ITSM is to understand how to use it within their organizational context.

This is the primary reason for this book: to show the business customer of ITSM how to do the same.

CHAPTER 1

ITSM 101: From Data to Wisdom

One of the enormous benefits of ITSM is that it teaches us to look at information in a different way. During the course of conducting business, we generate massive amounts of data. Technology can manipulate data into many forms of intelligence. We see examples of that every day, such as the way retail businesses track customer spending habits and use the data to analyze what they buy and when. This data, when examined in the context of buying patterns, helps them to understand the customer better and to sell more products. This is an example of using data as a tool for gaining wisdom about what customers value and will spend money on. ITSM practices teach us to decide what information is important to gather (as opposed to just collecting it because we can) and what decisions can be made with the information and how that adds value to the business. For example, we can track the way that customers use IT services and create better ways to manage product and service demands to align to customer habits. This is what we refer to as using ITSM to create value from data by seeing its potential as wisdom. To get there, we must first paint a picture of how ITSM is structured to accomplish this.

ITSM—Grass Roots

Successful businesses have common structural characteristics that are organized within levels of management hierarchy. Using a simplified form, the basic structural elements are as follows:

- **Corporate Strategy**—Direction setting and overall decision authority for business growth and health.

- **Governance**—Senior management policy, culture, and ethical guidance for the way a company will manage itself.

- **Compliance and Audit**—The policies, methods, and practices that ensure business operation adheres to legislative, corporate, and strategic requirements.

- **Operation**—The detailed process, function, activity, and work instruction information from which the business performs its role, and produces its product or service output.

These structural layers are surrounded by ongoing monitoring, measurement, and analysis that reveal strengths, weaknesses, vulnerabilities, and risks. Revealing these can catalyze changes to the structure that create improvement, better stability, and innovation opportunities for growth (see Figure 1-1).

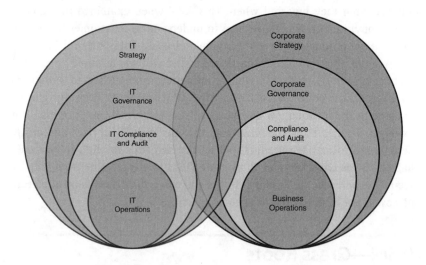

FIGURE 1-1   Business and IT structural elements

The structural elements of ITSM are linked to those of the business. The corporate strategy will set the basis on which the IT strategy is built, the corporate governance will direct the structure for IT governance, and so on. This means that from the very highest levels within the business, there is a need to recognize the partnership with IT and the need for alignment of corporate objectives and IT objectives. In order for IT to deliver quality, it must know what the organization values.

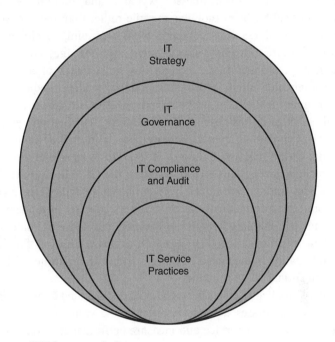

FIGURE 1-2   ITSM structural elements

ITSM—20/20 Hindsight

ITSM is used worldwide by large, medium, and small companies. It is recognized by standards organizations and is supported by an entire industry of ITSM-based products and services. Unequivocally, ITSM has proven its value in the past and continues to.

To best appreciate what ITSM is, it's important to understand a bit about its evolution. A few decades ago, as global economies began to have local impact on businesses, technology innovation was on the rise. The usefulness of IT to enable business potential was becoming more commonly practiced. The use of IT to automate business processes created a paradigm shift in business organizational models. Automation enabled businesses to do more with less human resource and cost and increased business intelligence potential by capturing more information about customer demands and behaviors. The exploitation of IT to provide better market share and competitive advantage for businesses exploded, and soon our dependence on IT as a critical business tool was the rule rather than the exception.

Within the business world, experts were beginning to create quality models to measure efficiency, effectiveness, and how they contributed to profitability or, perhaps more importantly, how a lack of a formalized quality model could inhibit profitability. Quality models, predictive analysis of consumer demand for products and services, became a critical element of successful business and maintaining competitive edge. The reliance on IT to capture metrics, analyze data, and provide such business intelligence meant that any failure of IT to perform its role in the business quality cycle would be far more devastating than a minor service disruption. Business leaders recognized a potential vulnerability—the risk of IT failure could now dramatically affect business success. In tandem, the IT innovations and enabling benefits to business drove the investment in IT higher than it had ever been. The reaction to this reality was for business to demand quality management initiatives within IT departments. This was the birth of formal ITSM thinking.

Initially, ITSM began emerging as a set of documented IT organizational functions and processes geared toward using a common language and activities to manage IT service and measure performance outputs in quality terms. The first emerging framework was ITIL®.[1]

ITIL is the worldwide-accepted framework for best practice in ITSM and remains at the heart of ITSM today. ITIL has undergone an evolution that continues as emerging technology, quality management expertise, and business complexity grows. Its current best practices revolve around lifecycle management of IT services and continue to be enabled through a collection of service management, customer-centric-focused processes that are measured in business value terms.

ITSM itself, like business quality models, is based on continual improvement and refinement; soon after the initial iterations of ITIL were embedding themselves in ITSM, the need for additional ITSM practices emerged.

The basic structural elements remain the same, and are now supported by more robust, mature practices that together create a synergistic body of knowledge for ITSM. Figure 1-3 provides a few examples of ITSM frameworks.

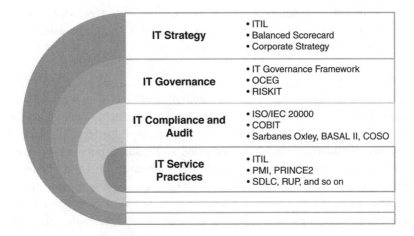

IT Strategy	• ITIL • Balanced Scorecard • Corporate Strategy
IT Governance	• IT Governance Framework • OCEG • RISKIT
IT Compliance and Audit	• ISO/IEC 20000 • COBIT • Sarbanes Oxley, BASAL II, COSO
IT Service Practices	• ITIL • PMI, PRINCE2 • SDLC, RUP, and so on

FIGURE 1-3   Some examples of ITSM frameworks

The evolution of ITSM into what it is today has spawned many additional frameworks that complement the ITIL framework. Most are developed by a consortium of ITSM industry experts and are refined into evolving best practices through maturing use.

The purpose of the illustration is to give examples of frameworks and methods more commonly in use within an ITSM practice, and it is not all-inclusive. An expanded list of ITSM-related frameworks and links to further information is included at the end of this book.

The ITSM industry is global, very mature, and supported by user organizations, vendors, experts, and research; it is continually expanding its frameworks and resources.

Here, we will focus on the basic elements within the better-known and accepted frameworks and methods. This will set the backdrop for understanding how to select the ITSM elements that meet your business needs and then negotiate them with IT providers to exploit a strong ITSM framework that will empower your business.

IT Governance

A governance system is all the means and mechanisms that will enable multiple stakeholders at various levels of an entity for specific purposes to have an organized say in setting direction and monitoring compliance and performance so as to create for them acceptable value, while taking acceptable risk levels and using limited resources responsibly. (Institute, 2010)

This is a generic definition of governance that fits any organization. IT governance is identical in its intent, method, and objectives. Without corporate governance, companies create difficult situations for themselves. We, unfortunately, see at the highest levels of business, the effects of a lack of governance. Take for example the experience of global economies that have been thrown into chaos when the proper governance of world economic powers is not intact. Within individual companies, the catastrophic effects of the absence of governance can also be seen. The purpose of governance, whether it is corporate or IT governance, is the same—to establish the rules of engagement for how the entity (in this case, the IT organization) will be operated.

Legislative compliance is often derived first from a lack of governance that creates a catastrophe, followed by law to enforce behavior and actions. IT governance should be a sub-element of overall corporate governance in which the business is clear about its style of policy and organizational structure that will extend itself to IT.

In the late 1990s, the IT Governance Institute[2] was established to stimulate international thinking around standards and methods for controlling enterprise IT investment decision-making, risks, and ensuring that business goals were met.

As a result, the industry has recognized the importance of establishing IT governance and its links to overall corporate governance. There are now many valuable best practices within the ITSM industry to set up and manage IT governance. A key outcome is the necessity for business and IT to create a partnership in the planning and execution of IT governance. Although this book will not discuss the intricacies of IT governance in any more detail than it will discuss detailed underpinnings of ITSM, some key knowledge in how IT governance affects the ITSM partnership is important.

IT governance directs the IT investment and therefore needs to be aligned to business governance and IT strategy. IT governance will dictate some rules of engagement on service provision; thus, businesses must consider this within the service management provision they are considering.

Governance Domains

In simple terms, IT governance is about the delegation of authority to a governing body to manage and establish policy by the organization's owner/stakeholders. Within IT governance, there are several key areas (known in the ITSM industry as *domains*) within which the governance activities are logically organized (see Figure 1-4).

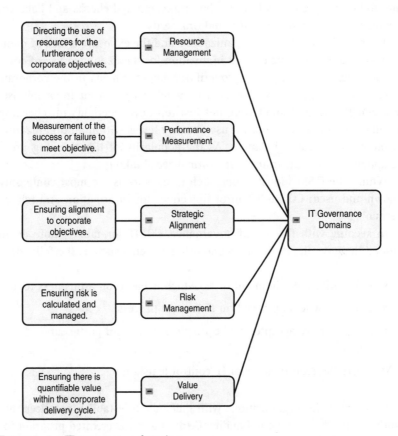

FIGURE 1-4   IT governance domains

IT Compliance and Audit

For many organizations, governance exists at more than an arm's reach away from where the work gets done. Although its importance is rarely questioned, how it is kept in touch with the operational levels of business is important. Think back to the days of Enron and the resulting legislation that followed, and you will agree that organizational checks and balances are intrinsic to corporate health and prosperity.

The complexity of many organizations and the exposure a lack of managed control could have created innovation for the expanded use of compliance and audit as a tool for identifying improvements in the corporate safeguards and raised awareness. This validated the need for a mindset that compliance and audit were not just top-down methods for checking up on operations, but a tool for use at many levels within an organization to mature checks and balances. As the popularity of this thinking grew, compliance and audit frameworks formalized thinking.

Within the ITSM industry, one such framework is the most commonly known and used: COBIT[3] (Control Objectives for Information and related Technology).

In keeping with the use of governance, COBIT formalizes more detail around the governance domains and offers benefits such as the following:

- Helps with the alignment of IT, which is based on a business focus.
- Defines ownership based on IT control process.
- Are generally accepted audit practices with third parties and regulators.
- Meets the requirements of IT control legislation.

COBIT provides organizations with guidance to establish practices that will meet the rigor of formal audits. COBIT has an accredited program for training COBIT auditors, which is flourishing in the ITSM industry as the popularity for compliance and control grows.

COBIT[4] is based on using business goals to define and relate IT goals to processes and activities. It is accepted practice and easily integrated with other ITSM methods to form part of a larger body of ITSM practice. The domains of COBIT are as follows:

- Plan and Organize:

  1. Define a strategic plan.

  2. Define the information architecture.

  3. Determine the technological direction.

  4. Define the IT processes, organization, and relationships.

  5. Manage the IT investment.

  6. Communicate management aims and directions.

  7. Manage IT human resources.

  8. Manage quality.

  9. Assess and manage IT risks.

  10. Manage projects.

- Acquire and Implement:

  1. Identify automated solutions.

  2. Acquire and maintain application software.

  3. Acquire and maintain technology infrastructure.

  4. Enable operation and use.

  5. Procure IT resources.

  6. Manage changes.

  7. Install and accredit solutions and changes.

- Deliver and Support:

  1. Define and manage service levels.

  2. Manage third-party services.

  3. Manage performance and capacity.

  4. Ensure continuous service.

  5. Ensure systems security.

  6. Identify and allocate costs.

  7. Educate and train users.

8. Manage service desk and incidents.

9. Manage the configuration.

10. Manage problems.

11. Manage data.

12. Manage the physical environment.

13. Manage operations.

- Monitor and Evaluate:

  1. Monitor and evaluate IT performance.

  2. Monitor and evaluate internal control.

  3. Ensure compliance with external requirements.

  4. Provide IT governance.

Within each of the domains, a series of cyclic activities (listed previously) define the management and flow of governance and compliance control. These are applied within the detailed governance areas (refer to Figure 1-4). The industry has recognized COBIT strengths, and it is used and recognized formally as a tool for conducting IT control and management audit.

International Standards

Many recognized best practices eventually have formalized standards that document the application of the practices in an auditable way. ITSM is no exception to this. A series of standards have emerged in support of ITSM and its various areas of practice.

The International Organization for Standardization[5] (ISO) is a network of National Standards Institutes with a central secretariat that coordinates the ISO system of standards development.

One of the better-known standards is the Quality Management Standard ISO 9001:2008. This has been used by businesses for years to demonstrate their quality practices. In a similar vein, the ITSM industry recognizes a series of IT-related management and leadership standards, such as the following:

- ISO/IEC 20000:2005—Standard for IT Service Management.

- ISO/IEC 27000—Information security management systems—Overview and vocabulary.

- ISO/IEC 27001—Information security management systems—Requirements.

- ISO/IEC 27002—Code of practice for information security management.

- ISO/IEC 27003—Information security management system implementation guidance.

- ISO/IEC 27004—Information security management—Measurement.

- ISO/IEC 27005—Information security risk management.

- ISO/IEC 27006—Requirements for bodies providing audit and certification of information security management systems.

- ISO/IEC 27007—Guidelines for information security management systems auditing.

- ISO/IEC 38500—The governance of management processes relating to the information and communication services used by an organization.

Each of these defines auditable standards for IT management and security practices, and many IT organizations will strive to achieve compliance to these as a means to illustrate their viability as IT service providers and adherence to industry practices.

Many businesses will look to acquire IT services only from providers who have achieved compliance to ISO 20000. The need for this is often merely a matter of preference, and there is no clear right or wrong, but understanding a bit about what ISO 20000 states can help any business look for the right things in a provider, or aspire its IT organization to work toward.

The importance of an ITSM standard has been illustrated by the upswing in acceptance and use of ITSM best practice frameworks shortly after the release of any of the ITSM-related standards. Many organizations will use the existence of a standard to validate the importance and therefore adoption for them of related best practices.

ISO/IEC 20000:2005 comes in five parts, as follows:

- Specification—This part promotes an integrated process approach to effectively deliver managed services. Coordinated integration and implementation of the service management processes provides the ongoing control, greater efficiency, and opportunities for continual improvement.

- Part 1 sets out the activities that are organized as a management system that outlines the basic elements of service management that must be done. It promotes the adoption of an integrated process approach to effectively deliver managed services to meet the business and customer requirements. It comprises ten sections:

  - Scope

  - Terms & Definitions

  - Planning and Implementing Service Management

  - Requirements for a Management System

  - Planning & Implementing New or Changed Services

  - Service Delivery Processes

  - Relationship Processes

  - Control Processes

  - Resolution Processes

  - Release Process

- Code of practice—Depicts an industry consensus on guidance to auditors and offers assistance to service providers planning service improvements or to be audited against part 1.

- Guidance on scope definition—For service providers to meet conformance with part 1, or for service providers who are planning service improvements and intending to use ISO/IEC 20000 as a business goal.

- Process reference model—This describes the processes including the general service management system processes implied by part 1. Each process of this model is described using a purpose and outcomes.

- Exemplar implementation plan—This provides guidance to service providers on how to implement a service management system to fulfill the requirements of part 1.

ITIL Service Management Practices

The oldest and best-known ITSM framework is ITIL. Accepted worldwide as the de-facto standard for ITSM, it remains the most widely used framework of its kind. It has evolved with business and IT over its 20-plus-year life, and currently is set within a service lifecycle context and is documented within five core volumes of best practice guidance and numerous complementary publications.

Considered by many to be operationally focused, ITIL tends to pick up where governance and compliance leaves off, and its practices are targeted strongly toward the day-to-day operation of service management within an organization. ITIL, like other frameworks we have discussed, relies on organized processes that define roles, activities, functions, inputs, and outputs for the flow of ITSM activities. ITIL processes interact and flow within a service lifecycle that begins as Service Strategy and moves through the stages of Service Design, Service Transition, and Service Operation, which are anchored by Continual Service Improvement (see Figure 1-5).

Each stage of the ITIL service lifecycle is fed by the others, and the processes are integrated in a logical way that follows the cycle of services. Briefly, the flow looks something like Figure 1-6.

The overarching premise of ITIL is the concept that ITSM must be measured in terms of how it provides business value. Every service and every IT management activity is ultimately measured in this way. This is why it remains the world's best-accepted framework for ITSM.

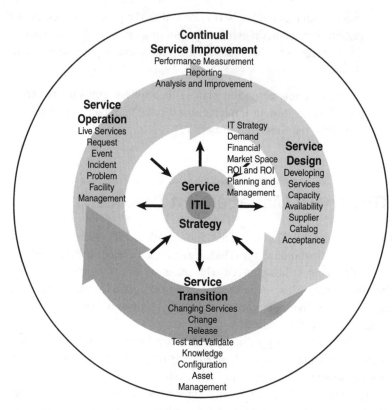

FIGURE 1-5   ITIL service management lifecycle

FIGURE 1-6   ITIL lifecycle flow

A simple way to illustrate how ITIL creates business value is shown in Figure 1-7.

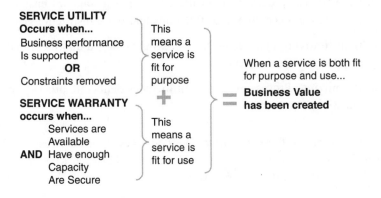

FIGURE 1-7   Business value creation with ITIL

Maturing ITSM practices

An integral part of an ITSM program is in understanding how ITSM practices are maturing within an organization. ITSM practices are designed to be adapted, improved, and matured over time, and the ITSM industry offers a few methods to measure how and maybe more importantly "if" an organization is maturing over time. Maturity methods have basically the same structure, and maturity is based on a five-level scale that corresponds to typical organizational practice traits.

The importance of maturing cannot be overstated. As ITSM practices mature, they tend to provide increasing benefit to the entire organization and the cycle of creating innovation and improvement becomes easier, more rapid, and useful. Every ITSM program must include some means of self-reflection for effectiveness, maturity, and improvement.

The five levels are defined along the maturity scale, and the predictability, effectiveness, and control of an organization's processes are believed to improve as the organization moves up these five levels:

1. **Initial (chaotic, ad hoc, individual heroics)**—The starting point for use of a new process.

2. Managed–The process is managed in accordance with agreed metrics.

3. Defined–The process is defined/confirmed as a standard business process, and decomposed to functions and work instructions.

4. Quantitatively managed–The process is managed and measured for effectiveness.

5. Optimizing–Process management includes deliberate process optimization/improvement.

Within each of these maturity levels are Key Process Areas (KPAs), which further characterize that level of maturity. For each KPA, there are five definitions identified, as follows:

1. Goals

2. Commitment

3. Ability

4. Measurement

5. Verification

In summary, successful ITSM frameworks typically incorporate strategy, governance, compliance, standards, and service practices that are performance measured for efficiency, effectiveness, and growing maturity.

This approach is often used by businesses wanting a comprehensive ITSM program. These frameworks have synergy and complementary aspects that strengthen their value when combined. The next chapter explores how these frameworks can help empower your business and improve your bottom line.

Endnotes

1. ITIL® is a Registered Trademark, and a Registered Community Trademark of the Office of Government Commerce, and is registered in the U.S. Patent and Trademark Office. IT Infrastructure Library® is a Registered Trademark of the Office of Government Commerce.

2. IT Governance Institute, 3701 Algonquin Road, Suite 1010, Rolling Meadows, IL 60008 USA.

   ISBN 1-933284-14-5, IT Alignment: *Who Is in Charge?*, Printed in the United States of America.

3. IT Governance Institute—COBIT 4.1.

4. 1996–2007 IT Governance Institute, COBIT, 4.1, Excerpt, Executive Summary Framework.

5. The International Organization for Standardization.

CHAPTER 2

ITSM: The Business Asset

A major advantage of using ITSM is the way in which it allows us to exploit assets for value creation. What is sometimes forgotten or not seen is that ITSM itself is an asset to the business because of its potential to contribute to maximizing the bottom line. Even though ITSM may not be the revenue-generating product, except if you happen to be a service provider who offers that, it does affect the business profitability in a positive way. This chapter looks at the things we need to have within an ITSM program that enables it to create value and improve the bottom line.

To help you be an effective negotiator with your IT service providers, this and following chapters will have a few aids:

- **A-ha moments**—These enlightening lessons you should keep bookmarked to help you harness the power of ITSM to your business benefit.

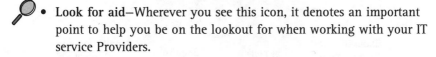

- **Lingo Lessons**—Tips that help you understand some key ITSM terms that will be valuable in your conversations with IT service providers and the context in which they are used.

- **Look for aid**—Wherever you see this icon, it denotes an important point to help you be on the lookout for when working with your IT service Providers.

The Roadmap

Now that you have a basic idea of the structure of ITSM and how it exists within a corporate framework, let's look at what each of the structural elements provides to business and how you can exploit them for business profitability.

The basic arsenal of ITSM for any organization contains the following, shown in Figures 2-1 and 2-2:

- **IT Strategy**—Direction and service design standards, which are linked to enabling business strategy and plans. These are forward-looking plans that articulate how IT will help enable business strategy.

- **IT Governance**—Established policy for management and controls of IT. Generally, it will align with corporate governance and organizational management. In cases where the IT organization is internal, the corporate and IT governance should always be aligned.

- **IT Standards**—Alignment to a standard if auditable compliance is required for legislative or management needs.

- **IT Service Practices**—The execution layer of policies, processes, function, and working-level detail to manage, monitor, execute, and improve IT-enabling technologies that support business process.

FIGURE 2-1   Basic structure

Figure 2-2 expands on the basic structure, lists some industry frameworks, methods, and bodies of knowledge that are commonly used, often together within a holistic ITSM program.

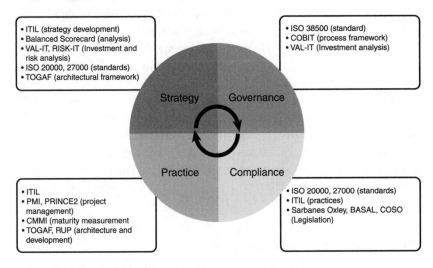

- ITIL (strategy development)
- Balanced Scorecard (analysis)
- VAL-IT, RISK-IT (Investment and risk analysis)
- ISO 20000, 27000 (standards)
- TOGAF (architectural framework)

- ISO 38500 (standard)
- COBIT (process framework)
- VAL-IT (Investment analysis)

Strategy   Governance

Practice   Compliance

- ITIL
- PMI, PRINCE2 (project management)
- CMMI (maturity measurement)
- TOGAF, RUP (architecture and development)

- ISO 20000, 27000 (standards)
- ITIL (practices)
- Sarbanes Oxley, BASAL, COSO (Legislation)

FIGURE 2-2   Frameworks that are often used together

Just as your business is built on a solid foundation of strategy, vision, capability, and execution, your ITSM needs must take their cue from your business needs. In order to create business requirements for ITSM, you must understand what business outcomes you are vested in, the direction your business is moving in, and how IT enables the execution of your business processes. Taking the time to articulate that and mapping them to ITSM capabilities will ensure that your IT Service Provider (ITSP) has the ITSM foundation that you need, what it must be capable of, how much of an investment it should take, and what return on that investment you should expect. An ITSP can be considered to be any IT providers you interact with to get IT services. This can include your internal IT department, external providers or any combination thereof.

IT Strategy

Whether you have an internal IT organization, outsource IT services, or use a combination of these, every business should require that the organizations that provide IT services to them have an IT strategy. Its purpose is to articulate the vision, direction, and how it will organize its capabilities and resources in order to support your business outcomes.

Often, a business's IT strategy will form part of a larger formalized business strategy, and this helps to ensure that the ITSM needs are aligned and integrated with the overall business goals. Considering ITSM as a lifecycle, it makes good sense to use IT strategy as the starting point to engage with your IT organization or IT service providers. Strategy is the fulcrum from which the nature and quality of service is directed.

Successful businesses consider themselves to be integrated with IT. Successful IT organizations consider themselves to be integrated with the business. Suppliers within a supply chain consider themselves integrated with each other. In every business there is a supply chain and this makes integration one of the most important aspects of good IT service. Each knows that the relationship is one of partnering from every point in the lifecycle.

What to Look for in an IT Strategy

There are many ways to articulate an IT strategy. For the business, the focus is on satisfying themselves that the IT organization understands the business needs and has a plan to support these. A good IT strategy will articulate this, and you should be able to see this throughout the strategy documentation. Some key areas to check for are the following:

- The list of business outcomes that IT is expected to support. This should be provided by the business.

- Articulated understanding of the underlying business processes that support business outcomes.

- A reference to a list of business services.

- Calendarized lists of IT planned, existing, and sun-setting IT services linked to business services.

- Awareness of the criticality within key business services.

- Connection between the management plans of IT and the support of business goals and outcomes.

- Recognition of the cycle of business change and how IT will keep pace and anticipate needs.

- How the IT organization will interact with business.

The preceding list is appropriate for internal organizations and external IT organizations that create an IT strategy for a particular business customer or customer type.

For IT service providers (ITSP) who deal with many business customers, their IT strategy might not be as specific about a particular customer's business goals or outcomes, but there are still things you should look for, either by asking to review the IT strategy, or by discussing it in general terms with the ITSP. Often, external ITSPs might be reluctant to share the actual documentation with you for reasons of proprietary commercial sensitivity and security; however, the ITSP should be quite willing to discuss their method of planning to meet customer needs and enable business outcomes.

Such a discussion is very valuable as it can quickly tell you whether the service provider actually understands their own strategy and if it is part of how they normally operate or a means to gain your business.

 Look for the following:

- Description of how the ITSP will engage with you as its customer to understand your business needs and expectations.

- How they will periodically review these and how they will prepare for unexpected business changes that they must support.

- How they prepare for planned changes to business needs.

- Which roles within the ITSP organization are accountable for ensuring the IT strategy, particularly those areas that relate to supporting the business customer, and the level of authority these roles have and how they are accessible to you as a customer.

- How the ITSP will monitor and measure the successful outcomes related to you as a customer and how they review customer satisfaction to improve.

For an example of an IT strategy, please refer to Appendix A, "Templates," later in this book.

Defining Business Services—Enriching the IT Strategy for Business Benefit

The business can be a catalyst for forming a solid IT partnership by being prepared to provide input into the IT strategy. The best way for an ITSP to meet your expectations is to sufficiently understand your business. Within the business/IT partnership, it is a business responsibility to articulate this understanding to the ITSP. Think about this as you would a catalog of services you would provide to your customers in order to illustrate what you offer them.

These fall into three basic categories, as follows:

1. Products or services delivered to your customers.

2. Products or services consumed by your staff.

3. Products or services consumed by both customers and staff.

These categories will depend on IT services and form your overall business requirements for ITSM. From an ITSM perspective these categories represent IT services. The nuances lie in the criticality of these to business performance and the impact to the business should any of the technology underpinning these services fail.

TABLE 2-1   A Typical Example of Business Services

Business Service	Description	Level of Significance (Criticality to Business)	Normal Hours of Usage During Regular Business	Atypical Usage During Exceptional Business Cycle
Online catalog	Product catalog for online customer purchases. Available globally in multiple languages.	High	24 hours daily	November to January for holiday rush and exchanges
Retail sales systems	Point-of-sale terminals in retail outlets. Available in 200 retail locations in 3 countries.	Critical	During retail outlet business hours of 9:00 am–9:00 pm (local time zones apply)	November to January for holiday rush and exchanges (extended hours of operation apply locally)
HR management system	Internal corporate use—HR management for employee documentation processing and staff evaluation.	Medium	During corporate head office business office hours (9:00 am–5:00 pm CST, Monday to Friday)	Critical on the 30th of each month for senior management reporting

Business Service	Description	Level of Significance (Criticality to Business)	Normal Hours of Usage During Regular Business	Atypical Usage During Exceptional Business Cycle
Employee payroll management system	Internal staff use—for logging timesheets, vacations, illnesses, benefits, and staff requests. Generates payroll calculations and deposits.	High	During corporate head office and retail outlet hours of operation (24 hours daily)	Critical during payroll processing bi-weekly on Thursdays
Email	Internal corporate use and external marketing and customer relationship use.	Critical	Regular hours of business operation and marketing campaign overnight launches (local time zones apply)	During regular monthly product marketing launch periods, and October to December for seasonal marketing campaign
Inventory control	Internal corporate use and external product supplier use. Automatically tracks inventory use from retail point-of-sale terminals and internal supply requisitions and sends orders to appropriate suppliers for inventory replenishment.	Critical	24-hour operation	Critical during seasonal retail inventory planning

A simple list of business services like the previous example provides an enormous amount of intelligence to the ITSP about what your service needs are and how they need to fulfill them using ITSM. This strengthens their IT strategy and their ability to meet your needs. Of course, this is not an all-inclusive list, but the general idea is to take the time to think about what your business services are. Many businesses will realize that, while going through this process, they have services they did not understand well themselves or had even identified as business services.

The IT version of this will be much more complex and will link the individual IT infrastructure elements—such as hardware, software, applications and data, support levels, and costs of service provision—to each of your business services. In ITSM, this is known as a Service Catalog and will follow on from an IT strategy to further define how IT services will be provided to the business. The Service Catalog is embedded within the service portfolio and is the portion of the portfolio reflecting live services the business can actively use.

> ## SERVICE CATALOG
>
> This is a term used within the ITIL best practices and the ITSM industry to depict a listing of services that an IT service provider offers to a customer. It is written in business terms and contains some standard information. Chapter 3, "The Service," Table 3.1 provides an example of Service Catalog Information.

Imagine how much margin for error or misinterpreted expectations there would be if the ITSP did not understand what your business services are and how critical they are for business operation.

Consider this. This simple list of business services forms the basis of everything else that follows, including

- The level of response you can expect to recover from service disruption

- How technical changes that affect your services are managed and when

- When business services are available and when they are not

- What the impact of service failure is to your business

- How much your IT services will cost, who pays, and in what form

- The level of security required

- The type of compliance and audit needed

- The governance policies that apply

- What return on value and investment you can expect

- How you can lower your cost and increase your profit

Although this seems straightforward and you think you've got it covered, let's take a closer look at how interpretation can change things. A service provider might look at the list of example business services in Table 2-1 and form a basic understanding of needs, but will likely require further clarifications, such as:

"We still aren't clear on availability. The list mentions three countries and local time zones. What countries and what time zones?"

"We aren't certain what you mean by extended hours? Is it a half hour, 24 hours, or something in between?"

"The list mentions bi-weekly, but which week is which? With whom is this agreed?"

This is a great example of what often happens between the suppliers and the customer. The customer thinks they have been explicit, but they haven't understood how literal an interpretation the stated requirements will go through. This teaches us that we need to develop requirements, and then have a dialogue to see how they are interpreted *before* they are agreed upon. You can surmise what could result if no further dialogue occurred in the previous example.

A-ha Moment

The ability to articulate your business services to your IT service providers is the single most important first step in creating the basis for successful ITSM. It can make or break the success of how your business services are managed and how your customers perceive the quality of them. Articulating business services and how they are used becomes the essential foundation of how the IT service provider forms the IT strategy.

Service Portfolio—Expanding the Horizon for Business-Centered ITSM Needs

A logical next step is to tie this into the corporate business strategy by articulating future business directions and the services that will likely come about as a result of business growth. Creating a similar list of planned services or initiatives can help the IT service provider incorporate business strategy into IT strategy and consider how business directions will shape IT future needs. It can also reveal cost-saving opportunities along with technology innovations that can create more robust and faster-to-market business services. This is the beginning of the business and IT partnership where service innovations, economies of scale, service asset exploitation, and market space innovation can accelerate business profits and increase business market share to new levels. Within ITSM, this is known as Service Portfolio Management.

At the formative stages of this process, a partnership between business and IT emerges, and each party begins to reformulate a common understanding and a common language of what services are.[1] Each party begins to understand the needs of the other, the necessity to maintain a dialogue, and the realization that ITSM is about enabling business outcomes. In this collegial environment, both business and IT have business outcomes that are integrated, harmonized, and create synergy for both sides of the partnership.

To catalyze a service portfolio, the partnership evaluates market spaces and creates a view of where business services will best serve their customer markets, create new markets, and generally define where the business is heading. This then provides the IT service provider with a roadmap with which they can evolve their IT strategy and refine service provision requirements. This is often a good point to begin thinking about business patterns of usage and how current and future business services are consumed by the customer. This drives investment decisions and service needs to a new level of efficiency by viewing services as a portfolio with interdependent parts and opportunities to leverage existing investments within new services. By this time, many businesses will begin to see a pattern emerge that can establish a sense of Return on Investment (ROI) and cost avoidance or savings in how services are developed and operated.

From an ITSM perspective, this part of the roadmap refines what IT and customer assets are needed to provide services, how they can be exploited for effective cost of ownership management, and the inherent capabilities and resources that must comprise the assets.

This can also reveal new innovation possibilities for the business to gain competitive edge. The IT provider, through having a good grasp of their industry innovations, might see possible ways that the business can use this to their advantage in their market. This has an increased chance of happening if the provider has a thorough understanding of the business services and how your customers use your services.

> ### SERVICE PORTFOLIO
>
> This is a term used by IT to describe a set of processes that define the services being planned for, those in use, and those being retired. It is set within a context of business planning, identified needs, and financial viability.

Exploiting Service Assets

Service assets are not much different than IT assets, contrary to the images we conjure when we think of IT assets. The reality is that assets are not merely those we consider in the traditional sense—that have a depreciable financial value. Service assets are anything within the organization that either on their own or when combined have the ability to produce value for the company.

In ITSM terms, service assets generally have one of two characteristics that drive how they produce value:

> **SERVICE ASSET**
>
> This is a common ITSM term used to describe any asset of an organization that can on its own, or when combined with other assets, produce value in the form of goods or services.

- **Capabilities**—Typically, these are things such as management, knowledge, exierence, and processes. They tend to be considered somewhat intangible and are usually embedded within the organization. Capabilities are considered a service asset when they contain the ability to coordinate, control, and deploy resources within an organization, thereby contributing value.

- **Resources**—Considered tangible type assets, resources are used by organizations to produce value. They consist of such things as information, applications, infrastructure, systems, and financial capital. They are coordinated to produce value in the form of goods or services.

Table 2-2 contains things every company has. The grid illustrates the capabilities or resource characteristics each has and an example of how they contribute value. This is what makes them service assets.

Table 2-2   Service Assets and Their Contribution to Value

Service Asset	Capability or Resource	How This Asset Provides Value
Management	Capability—A system of leadership, policies, and incentives within an organization.	Coordinates, transforms, and directs resources to produce value.
Organization	Capability—Configures resources for carrying out specialized activities.	Combining resources such as people, processes, and infrastructure to produce a product or service.

Table 2-2   Service Assets and Their Contribution to Value

Service Asset	Capability or Resource	How This Asset Provides Value
Processes	Capability—Repeatable methods, procedures, and routines to direct the execution of activities. These may be informal business traditions as opposed to formal documented processes.	Exert coordination and control of the business environment and are the engine in value production. Informal processes tend to carry more risk that formal, defined, and documented processes.
Knowledge	Capability—Accumulated awareness, experience, and information that are applied to activities.	Produces policies, plans, architectures, intellectual property analysis, and creates momentum to carry out activities to create value.
People	Both—Enhance the knowledge and capability of the organization through perception, creativity, judgment, action, leadership, and communication.	Direct and execute the value-producing activities. They disseminate and create knowledge. They create, combine, and consume all other asset types.
Financial Capital	Resource—They exist in a variety of forms and support other assets.	This asset measures the economic performance and value of the organization and enables the ownership or use of all other asset types.
Applications	Resource—Tools and automation to support other assets. Exist as software, hardware, documents, scripts, or instructions.	Applications enhance the performance of processes and are supported by other assets, such as people. They are assets most easily recognized as a contributor to service.

The capabilities and resources that exist within each service asset are what ITSM uses to determine the best way to exploit assets for their maximum ROI. Service assets are what we use to create value, influence demand, and provide services. This can be applied no matter what type of service it is. Consider this list within a manufacturing, financial, retail, IT, or health business. It applies equally in terms of the type of assets the business has and their use to provide value.

A common ailment of the ITSM partnership is the failure to recognize that these assets require management from both sides of the Service Management partnership. For example, corporate culture is also a key service asset. It can also be a key service disabler if attitudes and behaviors do not support the service philosophy of a company. The business will have specific service needs that dictate how the ITSP needs to provide them. The ITSP, in order to meet service expectation, needs the business to

follow certain processes to avail themselves of a service. If the business customer does not follow the expected process, the provider is at a disadvantage and cannot provide the expected result.

For example, a customer buys and installs software on their computer but fails to notify the supplier who maintains it. This customer did not follow the agreed process of first notifying the supplier so that proper compatibility testing with the computer's business configuration could be done. The customer ends up with a computer that isn't working, the supplier is unaware of the new software, and troubleshooting is taking much longer than it should. This costs the business, the customer, and the supplier wasted time and money.

The best industry examples of ITSM failures involve the breakdown of expected roles and behaviors from both sides of the Service Management partnership. This means that part of getting good ITSM involves being a good customer. If the ITSM provider can lower your costs by offering a single point of service interface for your staff, failing to use it consistently raises the cost of service provision to both partners. What's worse, it causes the perception of service quality to be poor when it actually isn't.

This will be discussed in more detail later in the book when we consider designing services for maximum business profitability.

A-ha Moment

The business and IT partnership requires commitment from both sides to effect a positive ITSM outcome. Business roles, cultural attitudes, and resulting behaviors must be taken into account in the expectations and demands from ITSM. It is the management and the innovation of combining service assets in particular ways that produce value.

IT Governance—What to Look For

Most reputable ITSPs will have some form of IT governance in place. A primary purpose of this is to ensure that value can be gained from the investment made in IT and that risks are properly and systematically managed. There is evidence that IT investments tend to be reviewed less often and with less business rigor than other types of investments. There is more than a little irony in this, given the level of business dependence on IT and the growing proportion of the overall budget that IT accounts for. Consequently, attention to IT governance within this regard is growing as a result.

Although much of the detail of IT governance will not be of direct interest to the business customer, it is important that you validate the existence of IT governance in the organization and provide a sense of the corporate governance areas within your business that the ITSP should be aware of and aligned to.

Your provider's IT governance policies can tell you a lot about the provider and how aligned to your objectives they will be in the relationship. Look for indications of how their policies help protect you as a customer and create a good basis for a relationship.

Look for:

- If they have a policy to regularly review the risk profiles of their business customers of IT services

- How the ITSP will ensure alignment to corporate objectives

- How they govern themselves in a way that ensures alignment to your business outcomes

- Evidence that they have established policies governing legislative compliance

- An indication that they mandate performance measurement policies in their delivery areas

- Evidence that there is a formal Governance Board structure, mandate, and business input mechanisms

From an ITSM framework perspective, much of what falls beneath IT governance is the mechanics to execute the mandate and policy. It is critical that as a business customer, the IT organization knows what it is trying to achieve. Its IT governance and strategy are the best means to prove that their main objectives are to meet your needs and that this is built into their highest level policies and embedded in their culture. This ensures that you will get what you expect from your ITSP.

In the previous section, we looked at defining business services and the workings of a service portfolio. Using this as a basis, let's now define business outcomes. This is what you share with the IT Governance Board that, in part, drives their mandate.

Business outcomes are simple, yet powerful, statements that define the service requirement. Recall that the definition of a service has two characteristics, as follows:

1. Supports a desired business result

2. Removes a business constraint

Each business outcome statement should satisfy one and sometimes both of these in order to guide IT with a clear understanding of business need (see Table 2-3).

Table 2-3   Example of Outcome Statements for Business Services

Business Service	Description	Level of Significance (Criticality to Business Performance)	Business Outcome Statement	
			Supported Result	Constraint Removed
Online catalog	Product catalog for online customer purchases. Available globally in multiple languages.	High	Customers can purchase products and services online...	...in easy-to-follow and fast steps using numerous flexible payment options.
Retail sales systems	Point-of-sale terminals in retail outlets. Available in 200 retail locations in 3 countries.	Critical	Customers can purchase, exchange, or return goods and services in all retail locations...	...without disruption and long wait times.
HR management system	Internal corporate use—HR management for employee documentation processing and staff evaluation.	Medium	Employees can log shift times and submit vacation requests... Managers can evaluate and administer employee documents...	...regardless of location or time of day.

There is one additional characteristic that comes into play. When a business finds opportunities for improvements or requires changes to services as needs evolve, reviewing the statements of business outcome, business, and IT can enhance these existing outcome statements to stimulate ideas for service improvement opportunities.

Using the online catalog business service, let's apply a quality improvement to a business outcome:

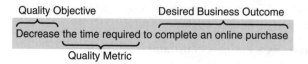

FIGURE 2-3   Business outcome improvement statement

Creating business outcome statements and quality improvement statements and linking these to regular reviews of how these are meeting actual business outcomes are an important contribution by the business to the ITSM partnership. The ITSP can use these to align the IT governance mandate and policies to business objectives and ensure that regular reviews incorporate quality improvements that keep time with business growth and change. These outcomes are further used in the deeper layers of ITSM to design, transition, operate, monitor, measure, and improve service quality to your business.

A-ha Moment

IT governance sets the playing field and rules of engagement for meeting business needs and managing risk. Providing business outcome statements and quality improvement statements are powerful ways for the business to contribute tangible value to the ITSM partnership and ensures that its needs are articulated properly and understood by the ITSP.

IT Compliance and Audit—Reasons to Have It

How do you know you are doing the right things and having the positive impact you intend? If your business has competitors, you know that at any time, you might be asked to prove *how* you are better. Within the IT world, proving service quality is a well-managed area of ITSM. For a variety of reasons, compliance and audit are fairly commonplace. Some of the better-known reasons are the following:

- Providing assurance to prospective customers that you meet an established standard of quality

- Proving that IT is operating within a secure environment

- Proving that business information and data is being protected in accordance with legislation

- Proving that IT practices are being followed according to their intended use

- Assuring business continuity in the event of disasters or catastrophic IT failure

As a business leader, you should require that your IT organization and ITSPs meet with industry compliance and audit standards and that their processes are subject to recurring checks and balances.

Safeguarding Business Integrity

Our dependence on IT for most of our business functions, such as storing and providing data and information, means that any loss of service or information that IT experiences can affect business integrity. ITSM practices are designed to safeguard business against such risk. This is a basic rule of IT governance, and the processes that ensure this are part of IT compliance, audit, and service practices.

Expect the Unexpected

What would happen to your business if a disaster struck and business-critical IT services were wiped out? How long would it take for you to have suffered irreparable damage and possibly a fatal blow to business survival? Good business practices will have business continuity plans for operating the various layers of the business should unexpected major events occur. For example, many companies have a policy that senior executives cannot all travel on the same airplane or in the same automobile, so that if an accident occurred, the entire senior management team could not be affected. Similarly, companies will have some safeguards in place to ensure continuity of operation in the face of unforeseen events.

IT Service Continuity Management (ITSCM) is an ITSM process, documented within ITIL, to create practices that ensure against irreparable business harm in the event of a disaster. Think of it as a business insurance policy. It's something you hope you never need but must have in place just in case you do.

ITSCM has four stages within the process, one of which is a direct business responsibility.

Stage 1

This is known as the "Initiation" stage. It extends itself to both IT and business and sets the continuity policies, terms of reference, and scope. It establishes the roles that all parts of the organization play. It is wise business practice to make available your business continuity plan to enable alignment.

Stage 2

This is the "Requirements and Strategy" stage. Again, the business has a direct role to play. The ITSCM Requirements stage creates a Business Impact Analysis (BIA) and risk assessment, which considers how damage or loss of business services might affect the business. For example:

- Lost revenue

- Additional costs

- Loss of competitive advantage

- Breach of legislation, contractual obligation, or health and safety

- Temporary or permanent loss of market share

- Corporate embarrassment

- Loss of shareholder confidence

- Loss of command and control of operation

The BIA quantifies this in two ways:

- **Impact**–The degree to which this will negatively affect the business

- **Time**–The time it will take for this impact to reach critical proportions

The "Strategy" part of stage 2 documents risk reduction measures and recovery options to support the business. No one but the business can possibly accurately define these parameters, and it is critical that you become involved in this part of ITSCM.

Stage 3

This is the "Implementation" stage. This is where IT takes over and produces its IT service continuity plans that align to your business continuity plans. Every ITSP should have this. For ITSPs who support many different customers, there will be generic parts to this plan and also some that might be customized for each customer or customer type.

 The business should satisfy itself that its ITSP has an ITSCM plan and look for things such as the following:

- Emergency response plan

- Damage assessment plan

- Salvage plan

- Vital records plan

- Crisis management plan

- Security plan

- Communication plan

You should also confirm that the ITSP has a test plan that periodically, at set and ad-hoc intervals, tests the ITSCM plan.

Stage 4

This is the "Ongoing Operation" stage. This stage ensures that regular awareness and communication of the ITSCM plan is reinforced within the IT organization and that it is reviewed on a regular basis and when business changes are implemented.

Check and Double-Check

As a business leader, you understand that your organization will be subjected to audits of your practices from time to time and that this is part of sound governance. The same is true for ITSM. Your business will invest large sums of its budget to IT and ITSM. It is important to receive assurances that this investment is achieving its goal and that the practices embedded in the IT organizations that support and operate it are being used as intended.

The ITSM industry uses established frameworks for this purpose, and one that is commonly used is COBIT (Control Objectives for Information and related Technology). The basic details of COBIT were related in the previous chapter.

As outlined in the COBIT domains, the audit focuses on the things we have been reading about thus far, and confirms that the ITSP is using them properly and can demonstrate this. All reputable ITSPs will conform to some recognized audit practice and should be willing to share some of the details with you as a customer.

COBIT, like ITIL, is process oriented and uses a matrix of interrelated processes to address various ITSM aspects. The business should require that its ITSPs are using audit controls and request evidence that the following things are being addressed:

- The IT and business strategy are aligned.

- IT risks are understood and managed.

- IT projects are delivered on time and budget and are meeting business goals.

- IT costs are optimized and services are aligned to business priorities.

- Service performance is measured and linked to business goals.

- Information security is in place and monitored.

It is no coincidence that this list covers the majority of what we have been learning and is the basis for a robust and strong ITSM practice.

The final layer in IT compliance and audit is IT standards. In the previous chapter, we covered what some of the ITSM-related globally recognized IT standards are. Although compliance to international standards is not compulsory for assuring the quality of an ITSP's service, it does establish a globally recognized baseline to measure against. As a business leader, the choice is yours whether you will require this level of compliance or not, but understanding the basics of what they are will help you determine the level of compliance you need.

It is important to distinguish how compliance standards such as ISO/IEC are applicable. First, the standards themselves are very generic. This means they can be applicable across a diverse user base, and they can be audited using industry standard audit methods. They are also applied to how the ITSP organization itself is managed, not their services. This is an important distinction and one that is often misunderstood. There is some assurance that an ISO-compliant provider will apply these standards to the services they provide, but it is not a mandated requirement.

Conforming to standards requires a program of regular audits, and this requires investment on the part of the organization. It is paramount for a business to determine if they need their ITSP to be standards compliant and with which standards.

To some degree, the ITSM industry works collaboratively; for example, the ITSM standard ISO/IEC 20000 is aligned well to governance and practice frameworks, such as COBIT and ITIL. For the business consumer, this is good news because requiring a vendor to comply with the ISO standard often means the ITSP uses COBIT, ITIL, or both.

IT Service Practices

As a business leader, you understand the importance of strategy, governance, and compliance. For the most part, you will want to be certain that your IT service provider incorporates these elements within their organization, but often this is out of the direct control of the business customer. If your business uses third-party IT service providers, you will want to investigate that your providers use strategy, governance, and compliance, but there will rarely be an occasion to negotiate the specific terms of such elements. IT service practices are where the rubber meets the road and where you need to focus on fit-for-purpose IT service provision for your business.

Most ITSM provisioning uses a combination of internal and external services. It's common for the internal IT organization to take on the role of managing third-party service providers; however, this is often an area where problems can occur if the IT organization does not clearly understand the business service needs. There are more than enough examples of internal IT organizations that do not understand business requirements alone!

It should not matter whether your IT services are provided internally or externally if you are knowledgeable about what you need and how to get it from IT. Most ITSM books are written for IT and start from a lower level of IT component detail and work their way up to a service. We are doing the opposite here: deconstructing a business service to identify what service artifacts you need to get the right service.

In the previous sections, we discussed how to articulate your business needs, define business services, and create business outcome statements and improvement statements. Here, we look at the basics of IT service practices that ITSPs use and what you need to know to develop a beneficial relationship with your ITSP.

Because ITIL is the globally recognized best practice and stands alone in this part of the ITSM spectrum, we focus on it as the basis for understanding and exploiting IT service practices for business profitability.

The Finely Tuned Engine of Business

It's a pretty safe bet that anyone reading this book has heard of McDonald's.[2] Started in 1940 and now a household name around the world, there is a reason that a McDonald's consumer is a loyal one—sustained and consistent customer experience. As a business, McDonald's is like any other. It produces products and services, it has competitors, it must change its services as consumer tastes change, and it relies on a complex supply chain and technology to deliver to customers.

McDonald's enjoys success for the same reasons that all successful companies do. No matter where you visit a McDonald's restaurant, you know what to expect. Your food will be served quickly, the staff will be courteous, and the facility will be clean. The menu will be familiar and the prices predictable. This predictability and familiarity breeds consumer confidence and loyalty. So, how does McDonald's achieve this sustained, predictable, and consistent service? By being process-driven and aligned to the needs of their customers.

What characterizes companies that are process-driven and aligned are traits you can look for in your ITSP as well. Consistent customer experience is essential. An ITSP will usually offer a service desk or a focal point of contact to accept customer inquiries for service, report service issues, or request service changes. Process-driven ITSPs will have predictable interaction methods with the customers. They will usually confirm caller details, solicit information about the issue or request, perform some initial triage for issues, and explain the process for handling your request. What makes them stand apart as high performers is the consistency of following a routine such as the one just described *every* time. In this way, the customer develops a sense of being well cared for and knows what to expect and what to provide to the service desk agent. A partnership-type relationship develops from this and contributes to a positive quality experience.

Behind the scenes of this encounter between the service desk and the customer is the ITSM engine at work. The service desk will use four basic ingredients configured in a specific way to generate this consistent customer-focused quality experience, as follows:

- **People**—Well-trained service desk staff who understand your business services and already have access to critical pieces of information about you as a customer, such as what services you use, what service levels you pay for, historical information about the issues or requests you have had prior to this, and scripted dialogue cues that help solicit consistent information. (Think about how you place an order at McDonald's. It's the same every time you do it.)

- **Process**—The service desk has specifically documented processes that are crafted to a work-instruction level for every type of issue or request likely to be encountered. (After your McDonald's order is taken, it is passed onto fulfillment teams the same way every time.)

- **Products**—The service desk uses technology that enables and enhances the execution of the processes used by the service desk agent and their interaction with you. For example, you might be able to log your own request using a support website, which automatically gets routed to the part of the ITSP organization that can fulfill it. The service desk agent might use a tool that shows them how all your services are configured and monitored to help investigate the likely cause of an issue or incident. (McDonald's uses intelligent point-of-sale technology that already has configured menu items that feed the fulfillment team with your order information.)

- **Partners**–The service desk likely makes use of a delivery chain of supply to fulfill your requests or resolve incidents that can be other more specialized areas of the ITSP or third-party fulfillment providers. (Your McDonald's order triggers inventory adjustments to ensure that the supply or products are always available for you as a customer.)

These four elements are the basis of what drive ITIL processes within an ITSM framework, and they are the reason that you can rely on a consistent quality experience.

Successful ITSPs know that sustained quality of service, a predictable customer-centric service philosophy, and a partnership approach to ITSM achieves customer loyalty and continued growth and prosperity. They also know what McDonald's does–that the key to sustained consistency is process-driven and focused on business outcomes. In this way, IT service practices represent the engine of business. How finely tuned it is, is a matter of practice maturity and the reason that many companies use best practices in the first place.

Don't hesitate to ask potential ITSPs what level of ITSM maturity they have and how long they have been using ITSM practices. There is a connection between longevity of use and maturity in most cases.

Every service has a lifecycle. and ITIL is built around that concept. ITIL processes revolve around the stages a service flows through during its life. From the moment the business articulates a need and establishes desired business outcomes, a service begins its journey from strategy through design, transition, operation, and into improvement.

What happens to a service during each of these stages determines what the ITSP needs to be in control of to manage it.

It's worth mentioning at this point that while the rigor of following established processes creates customer confidences and a consistent service experience, as in the McDonald's analogy, what is equally part of the successful customer experience is knowing when variations from the standard enhance the experience. McDonald's, for example, makes variations to small things that have a major impact on customers in various parts of the world. In Thailand sweet chili sauce is offered with food, in Brazil the coffee is stronger, and there is an absence of pork in countries where it is not consumed for religious reasons. All of these things require variation from standards, but only enough to customize the experience for a target customer.

Figure 2-4 shows what must be managed and controlled.

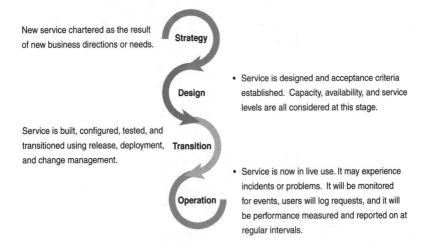

New service chartered as the result of new business directions or needs. **Strategy**

Design
• Service is designed and acceptance criteria established. Capacity, availability, and service levels are all considered at this stage.

Service is built, configured, tested, and transitioned using release, deployment, and change management. **Transition**

Operation
• Service is now in live use. It may experience incidents or problems. It will be monitored for events, users will log requests, and it will be performance measured and reported on at regular intervals.

FIGURE 2-4   A service experience through the lifecycle

It is during these stages of a service's lifecycle that the business can reap major benefits in negotiating the terms under which the service is managed. This is where the potential for increasing the ROI, lowering costs of managing, and tapping into innovations that improve business profitability occur.

The following table expands on Figure 2-3 and illustrates what the various parts of the service lifecycle means to the business and to the ITSP:

TABLE 2-4 Lifecycle Stages and Their Meaning to Business, IT, and Return on Investment

Lifecycle Stage	What It Means to the ITSP	What It Means to the Business	Business Benefit	How This Affects ROI
Strategy	• Trigger is business strategy. • Approved business case, and investment position are inputs. • High-level discussions with business about service requirements. • Service added to service portfolio pipeline.	• Interact with IT at the inception of needs. • Provide outcome statements to ITSP. • Agree service charter. • Trigger for review of strategy, governance, and compliance to account for new or changing service needs.	• Cost-managed service development. • Clarifying needs at the entrance level of service. • Conceptualizing engages the ITSP in a partnership approach. • Established ROI expectations.	• Establishes achievable expectations within the business-IT partnership about what is realistic, what the targets are, and the timeline for ROI to be achieved. • The business can understand true costs of service provision, and IT can understand the cost and priority for the business. • Simplifies investment decisions when accurate ROI information is trusted.

TABLE 2-4   Lifecycle Stages and Their Meaning to Business, IT, and Return on Investment

Lifecycle Stage	What It Means to the ITSP	What It Means to the Business	Business Benefit	How This Affects ROI
Design	• Triggered by a service charter. • The business will be active in establishing service requirements, which include functionality, performance, and service levels. • The business will articulate what business processes are using the service, how it will be used, and what the desired outcome is. • Review of IT architectures, management systems, measurements systems (design aspects) to look for innovation, scale economies, and shared service opportunities. • The ITSP will consider capacity, availability, configuration, and business usage patterns in design and produce the service acceptance criteria with the business.	• ITSP will engage business to clarify the outcomes needed. • Ability to participate in design criteria. • Agree service acceptance criteria with ITSP. • Establish service level requirements. • Consider sources of supply. • Create or revisit business continuity plans. • Consider design constraints, such as legislative compliance, costs of ownership, and so on. • Consider partnership or shared service opportunities with other business units, departments, or companies. • Opportunity to investigate innovation for additional services or market spaces.	• The business will have direct input into the design and development. • Share responsibility for success and acceptance criteria. • Service design will be accurate, more efficient, and likely to succeed on time and budget. • There is an increased rate of first-time acceptance and less fine-tuning changes or, worse, failed projects and services that do not meet the business need. • Business stakeholder buy-in at an early stage and ability to influence business cultural acceptance of changes. • Greater prediction of competitive edge with reliable delivery controls.	• Faster and greater ROI with fit-for-purpose and fit-for-use. • Faster time to market, and increased competitive edge and profitability. • Better planning horizon and strategic input for service demand and market competitiveness.

TABLE 2-4 Lifecycle Stages and Their Meaning to Business, IT, and Return on Investment

Lifecycle Stage	What It Means to the ITSP	What It Means to the Business	Business Benefit	How This Affects ROI
Transition.	• Triggered by a completed service design package or service change request. • The new or changed service is built, tested, configured, validated, and released for live use. • The ITSP uses this stage to also enhance the knowledge base for support and maintenance of the service and ensures that the business is prepared for the launch of the new or changed service. • Integrates service and project management disciplines in a manageable way.	• Smoother transitions. • Quick response to business needs and changes. • Greater depth of information management and growth of knowledge base. • Business requirements are built into the service using design specs that have been business-approved. • Changes or retrofits are better managed. • Ensuring business and IT readiness before release of new or changed service.	• Less downtime with better planned change timing. • Assurance that changes or newly developed services will meet business needs. • Transitional support during early operation. • Lower overall cost of managing changes with less re-work after implementation. • Lower risk of unexpected service breaks from improper or lack of rigor in testing. • Provides predictable, controlled changes to live business services.	• Cost-effective optimization of resource usage. • Increases speed of adoption and utilization of services. • Lowers overall cost of ownership. • Increases NPV with overall cost efficiencies. • Higher degree of meeting projected ROI with controlled management practices.

TABLE 2-4   Lifecycle Stages and Their Meaning to Business, IT, and Return on Investment

Lifecycle Stage	What It Means to the ITSP	What It Means to the Business	Business Benefit	How This Affects ROI
Operation	• Optimized processes for monitoring, operating, and measuring services. • Resource and role organization for better utilization. • Repeatable execution of service activities for consistent cause and effect. • Ability to measure customer perceived versus actual value.	• Focused service portal for accessing IT needs. • Published service levels with agreed fulfillment times. • Knowledge of the status of services in real time. • Being a service partner and using services as agreed. • Reviewing service performance reports with IT and discussing improvement opportunities.	• Efficiently managed services. • Improved service availability. • Assured and tested recovery in failure situations of any scale. • Resolution of requests and incidents in a timely way. • Confidence of consistent and agreed levels of service quality. • Ability to enjoy a true partnership with ITSPs that brings measurable value to the business.	• Ability to view balanced scorecard of IT service value to business at regular intervals. • Proactive, early, and consistently managed cause and effect of service disruptions that affect ROI. • Ability to project ROI changes based on service performance indications. • Ability to target improvements that increase ROI based on service performance. • Ability to track projected ROI to current and more quickly measure the effect on ROI from changes that are implemented.

In the next chapter, we'll learn how to use our knowledge of the lifecycle activities to business advantage when negotiating with ITSPs.

Endnotes

1. ITIL definition of service: "A service is a means of delivering value to customers by facilitating outcomes customers want to achieve without the ownership of specific costs and risks." Service Strategy

2. McDonald's Corporation, 2111 McDonald's Dr., Oak Brook, IL 60523

CHAPTER 3

The Service

Businesses that excel and stand apart are ones that understand how they provide value to their customers. They have defined their core services, and the entire focus of everything the company does ultimately can be tied back to delivering their core services with the quality, reliability, and value that their customers remain loyal to them for. Competent service management is a prerequisite for success and for business to be excellent, its service management must be as well. At the heart of ITSM is the concept of service. Unless it is clearly understood what services are being provided and used, service management becomes impossible. In business and in ITSM we have to understand what we intend to manage.

In this chapter, we look at the basic ingredients of services and service practices. We will also learn the basics of ITSM terminology to help shape our understanding of dialogue we need to have with IT Service Providers (ITSPs) to ensure service assets are exploited to the benefit of the business bottom line.

The Anatomy of a Service—Building the Services You Want

In the last chapter, we touched upon the concept of the service portfolio as an ingredient in service strategy with the intent of focusing on service investments. The service portfolio is the means to identify for the ITSP what you need now and will want in the future. There is a logical flow from here toward deeper detail and refined service needs that will shed

light on what type(s) of ITSPs you should be engaging with for service provision and management. You need to fill in the list of ingredients you must
have to build on in order to bring the portfolio to life.

We'll start with the basics and then develop an understanding that you
can build effective service management on. Within the anatomy of a service we'll examine how a service delivers value, the kinds of relationships
to seek with ITSPs for particular circumstances.

Along the way, we'll be using some ITSM terminology that will be helpful in having a dialog with ITSPs and useful during negotiations.

Service Ingredients

Every service has a basic list of ingredients, as follows:

- **Purpose**—What it exists for and the business processes it enables.
  This will be driven by the outcome statements you've created,
  which state what you need a service to do for you.

- **Functionality**—The things the service does for you that achieve its
  purpose. This is the service utility or what we refer to as fit for
  purpose.

- **Performance**—How well the service functions work to meet the
  purpose. This is the service warranty. This is measured in a variety
  of ways, which include availability, capacity, responsiveness, reliability, and so on.

- **Quality**—The overall perception of how valuable a service is to its
  users.

Our sense of how well a service is designed and operating for our needs
stems from how it is managed. This, of course, is an integral part of service management. Failure to properly manage a service will impact one or
all of these ingredients. So, to complete the picture, we have to add the
service management ingredients that ensure service is designed and managed to suit our needs. These are factors that affect overall business operation and ultimately the bottom line, so understanding the basics of
service management can maximize how well this is accomplished.

We'll Have What They're Having, Please!

The companies that leave lasting impressions on us are those that offer the kind of service experience that stands out. The trick to getting it is to understand what makes it stand apart from the ordinary, and how you as the customer play a role in making that happen.

Good service management should be relatively invisible to the business. Services should operate as expected, and no service disruptions should be experienced. When support is needed, it should be provided efficiently and effectively, and it should resolve issues the first time. This is typically what we think of as a good service experience.

It takes planning, capability, competence, resource, and harmonious partnering to have good service. This, of course, takes place behind the scenes and thus is what makes good service invisible to the customer.

In the prior chapters, you've learned how to define the services you need and what you need from them. The next step is to look at how those services need to be managed by the ITSP.

There are basic service expectations for service management and specific characteristics within a service that define why it is perceived as good quality for investment. Generally, these are as follows:

- The service does what you expect it to.

- The service operates reliably and is dependable over its life span.

- The service does not require many unplanned changes to keep its operations stable.

- Changes the business does require are preplanned and do not require extensive redesign.

- The service is cost efficient to operate and support.

- The service delivers the intended business outcomes.

- During periods of heavy use, the service continues to perform optimally.

- The service will scale to the evolving needs of the business.

When any of these fail, we perceive the service to be of poor quality. In fact, there are mainly only two reasons why a service is perceived as having poor quality:

1. The service's design does not meet the business needs.

2. The way the service is managed does not meet the business needs.

These are two key areas that ITSM practices are intended to address. Setting achievable expectations depends on a common understanding of what the service is, what it should do, how it will be managed, and how it will be measured.

We now know what ITSM is, and what a service is; next, we'll define the details that set and manage expectations for both the business and the ITSP.

A-ha Moment

To get good service, we need to keep only this small list in the back of our minds. The details are for negotiation and discussion with the ITSP. The details support the basic quality service ingredients. It's easy to get lost in the noise of details, many of which are not useful in defining the basic service needs and quality of how it's delivered. Keep your focus on the high-level ingredients and tie the details to those.

Service Catalog

The best way to avoid running into quality issues is to insist that your ITSP will provide you a service catalog. This is an articulation of what services offer and the terms and conditions that they are offered under. Your role is to help the ITSP define what should be in your catalog. The first rule of service catalog design that all good ITSPs know is to talk to the business customer.

Without a service catalog, it's difficult to know what services are available to you from the ITSP, and very difficult to discuss, measure, judge or even complain about them!

The following section takes the ITSM industry best practices guidance for the basic information that should be in the service catalog. Table 3-1 further explains what each of these mean and the effect this has on your business bottom line. Caution: The side effect of studying the list will be learning some basic terms in the ITSP's vocabulary. That could prove to be extremely helpful in negotiating the best service!

TABLE 3–1 Example of Basic Service Catalog Information

Service Catalog	What It Means	Who Provides It	How It Impacts the Bottom Line
Service Name	A uniformly understood descriptor to identify the service.	Business	Establishes the understanding between the business and the ITSP about what a service is considered to be.
Service Description	Describes (in business terms) what the purpose of the service is.	Developed jointly using the outcome statements provided by the business	Accurately sets out what the service must do. Saves time and money if done at the design stage. Some experts say it can cost 100 times more if left until after the service is implemented.
Service Category	This defines whether the service is part of a shared service, a core service, or a specialty service.	ITSP	Helps to exploit use of service assets in the most advantageous way and drives possible service models to be considered.
Standard Service Features	Describes features and functions of the service available to any employee who receives the service.	ITSP—This is derived from the outcome statements and service design package. Clarifies the costs associated with the generic service functions.	Clarifies the costs associated with the standard service.
Optional Service Features	Describes features and functions of the service available on special request and often with additional cost. This can also be optional features for specific business units.	ITSP—This is derived from the outcome statements and service design package and further improvement activities.	Clarifies and segregates costs for additional options and is useful as a planning tool for what is necessary and for whom.
Business Owner	Accountable business individual with whom the decisions rest for managing the service.	Business	Requires accountability to be documented and ownership managed.
Business Unit	The business customers who can use this service.	Business	Establishes access rights and ensures confidentiality of access to the data generated and used by the service.

TABLE 3-1   Example of Basic Service Catalog Information

Service Catalog	What It Means	Who Provides It	How It Impacts the Bottom Line
Service Manager	Accountable ITSP individual with whom the decision rests for ensuring the service delivers value. This individual will meet with the business owner on a regular basis as part of the service level agreement terms.	ITSP	Enforces accountability from the ITSP for the management point of contact for the service.
Service Hours	When the service operates and can be used by the business.	Jointly agreed by the business and ITSP	Directly impacts service costs and service availability.
Business Criticality	The dependence level the business has on this service to carry on business.	Business	Defines the cost to support, the level of support, and support response levels needed.
Business Priority	Defines any specific times during a business cycle when the business criticality changes.	Business	Drives support costs and ITSP windows of maintenance and change activities.
Business Contacts	Defines who the accountable contacts are for queries.	Business	Enforces accountable roles and responsibilities and the costs involved.
Escalation Contacts	Defines the contacts along the escalation path for the business and the ITSP in the event of serious service issues response.	Business and ITSP	Establishes reporting hierarchy in the event of service issues or failures and identifies accountability within both organizations.
Service Reports	Defines the type, frequency, and distribution of reports.	ITSP as agreed with the business	Contributes to the monitoring and measurement against expected norms and quality criteria. Identifies deviations and potential costs or savings.

TABLE 3-1   Example of Basic Service Catalog Information

Service Catalog	What It Means	Who Provides It	How It Impacts the Bottom Line
Service Reviews	Defines the structure for joint service reviews—details will be part of the service level agreement.	ITSP and the business	Post mortem of previous service cycle performance against agreed criterion. Can identify opportunities for further cost savings, improvements, and risk mitigation for the business.
Service Costs	Indicates unit costs for standard and optional features.	ITSP	Enables investment planning and costs analysis.
Service Targets	Defines the basic targets for availability, issue management, special requests, changes, and recovery from disruptions.	ITSP	Direct relationship to service cost, efforts, quality, and performance expectations. This is reflected in overall cost of service ownership.

The details within the service catalog are an extremely good snapshot of the areas for which the business must be able to negotiate the terms with the ITSP. A good practice for the business is to draft the terms of a service for itself in preparation for negotiation with ITSPs to help cover all relevant areas.

A-ha Moment

The service catalog is a primary resource in making sure you cover the important areas of what a service will look and feel like in use and how your ITSP will manage it. Without this you simply don't know for certain what you are paying for. A good practice is to create your own draft of a service catalog item to become familiar with what you will negotiate with the ITSP.

The Service Agreement

The next critical ingredient in every service is the service agreement (SA). This is also commonly called a Service Level Agreement or SLA. From a customer perspective, the SA defines the essence of service quality and the perception of ITSP performance in relation to that. This is where the art of negotiation with the ITSP is important. In terms of the business bottom line, the SA can have a great positive or negative impact to the business if it is unclear, ineffective, not followed, or breached regularly. Chapter 6, "The Service Agreement," is devoted to the detailed content and negotiation of the SA. It is important before you negotiate the terms of a SA, that you understand the ITSM terms and how they relate to the SA in order to be sure that the SLA you agree to is achievable and will work in practice.

- Service Desk—A service desk is a single point of contact for all your service needs. By having a single point of contact with your ITSP, you eliminate the need to troubleshoot problems yourself to determine the possible cause, and then know who to contact for help. A central premise of ITSM is that the customer should not have to troubleshoot a technical problem. This is the role of the ITSP, and the customer should only have to contact the ITSP to start the process. Every ITSP should offer a service desk. Many ITSPs will offer a variety of ways for making contact; via telephone, web, and fax are common.

- **Incident**—This is the term used to describe an unexpected occurrence with a service. The customer is experiencing something unusual. This could include not being able to access a program, a service is not responding as it normally does, or something has broken. Every ITSP must have an established process for managing incidents that should include conducting an initial investigation by having the customer describe the symptoms and determining the best means for dealing with the incident. This will often be done by the service desk agent either on the telephone, or using remote support technology to physically take control of the equipment.

- **Problem**—This is a term an ITSP uses to identify that a service has experienced multiple incidents of the same type for which the underlying cause is still unknown. Generally a problem is a recurring service issue that is still being investigated to decide how to fix it. Customers are helpful in reporting each incident they experience because it will quickly uncover a trend and might actually prevent a major service outage from occurring. Your ITSP should use a problem management process.

- **Service Request**—This is a process used by an ITSP for managing ad-hoc or predefined requests by the customer. These could include such things as moving computer equipment, creating a new user account, or buying new equipment.

- **Availability**—This term refers to the service being available for use by you. Generally, this will be documented within a service level agreement or service report and expressed as a percentage (98.0% available during a time period) or a period during a cycle (9:00 am to 5:00 pm Monday to Friday). This is important to you because most service quality issues stem from a lack of availability or unpredictable period of down time.

- **Capacity**—This term relates to the ability of a service to meet the size or volume needs of the customer without degraded performance. An example of this is an email account that is sized for 6 GB of storage. There is a direct relationship between capacity and cost. The ITSP should use a capacity management process to predict, based on your business usage and growth projections, what levels of capacity are needed, and when, before you suffer a service failure for lack of capacity.

- **Demand**—This term is used in two ways by an ITSP. First, it is used as a trending pattern of how business customers use services. This will generally be measured over a typical business cycle. Second, it is used in a technical way to measure and monitor business activity patterns against service capacity and potential uses for additional services or customers. It is a key element in capacity planning and service costing.

- **Service Level**—Likely one of the better-known and important terms for the customer, this term refers to the parameters of service quality the customer pays for and the ITSP ensures. Often, this will be expressed in a variety of ways, consistent with how service quality is viewed by the customer, such as response time for incidents or requests, hours of service availability, targets for measuring quality or satisfaction, parameters for making changes, and costs for the service.

- **Service Agreement**—This is commonly referred to as the SA and is the documented terms of the service levels for each service. An SA can include multiple services or a single service. There are industry practices for what should be included in the SA. The SA is often a quasi-legal document between the ITSP and the customer that stipulates how breaches of service are reported and dealt with.

- **Utility**—This term refers to the usefulness of a service for the customer. It refers to how fit for purpose a service is and is measured against the business need. It should be defined during the design stage and not after the fact.

- **Warranty**—This is the term used to describe the way a service performs against its intended design. It refers to how fit for use a service is.

- **Service Improvement Plan**—This term refers to how an ITSP prepares to improve service quality through a cycle of measuring performance, looking for opportunities to improve upon them, or to address a deficiency noted and agreed as such.

- **Service Portfolio**—This refers to a form of managing services that uses a strategic approach to viewing services as assets and investment strategies. Services are viewed as a whole and exploitation of assets for enterprise return on investment benefits.

- **Service Catalog**—The service catalog is part of the service portfolio that is a tiered view of the services offered to customers for use. The tiered view offers a technical view of how service assets are combined in various service models, as well as packages for exploitation across single or multiple customers. The service catalog will often be the platform for customer self-service portals.

- **Service Change**—This is anything that alters a service from its current state or needs to perform maintenance on a service. A service change can be requested by a customer or the ITSP. There is a cost involved for most changes. Your ITSP must use a change management process. Unauthorized and poorly planned and tested changes are the number-one cause of service failures and unplanned costs and lost revenue for the business.

- **Service Target**—This term refers to a level of measure for a service that is an agreed level. This can be applied to availability, reliability, time between failures, length of change windows and maintenance periods, response time for incidents, and service requests. Almost every facet of a service measure will have a target. The service target is the base against which actual performance and metrics are applied to determine overall performance of the service and the ITSP.

- **Escalation**—Periodically, a need for escalation will arise. This describes an established and agreed pattern for who should be involved and when. Escalation can be applied to service incidents and problems most commonly but also to most other service facets as well. Escalation generally identifies who, when, what, where, and how each level of escalation progresses.

- **Continuity**—Discussed briefly in Chapter 2, "ITSM: The Business Asset," service continuity refers to the planning and agreement of the impact to the business in the event of a catastrophic service failure and will have a detailed plan about how continuity is managed. Every ITSP should have a continuity plan for services.

- Reliability—This term generally applies to the level of stability that a service is expected to provide. A common metric for reliability is the average time between service incidents. It is used to measure overall performance of a service against the expected norms.

All of these terms are part of the IT service practices layer of ITSM and are where the meat of daily ITSM activities occurs. The list is a partial one that contains the more commonly used terms and those needed for dealing with ITSPs. You can find a full list of ITSM terms freely available on the web.

A-ha Moment

As a business person, you do not need to know extensive amounts of ITSM jargon or have detailed process knowledge to conduct effective negotiations with an ITSP or to create solid service descriptions that tell your ITSP what you need. A few basics are the key to a great dialog! ITSM is based on a common language using common terms. Any ITSP who doesn't know and use these terms should be avoided.

In the next chapter, we will begin looking at the anatomy of the ITSP. This is a good time to summarize a few key pieces of ITSM knowledge, as follows:

- ITSM is made up of governance, strategy, compliance, audit, and daily service practices. They are applied within a service lifecycle and are mainly a collection of interrelated processes, procedures, activities, roles, and responsibilities.

- ITSM looks slightly different in every organization, and the key is adapting best practices to fit your business needs.

- ITSM is as important to your business as it is to the IT service provider. It saves money, reputations, and even entire companies.

- Services are reflections of business needs that are driven by desired outcomes and managed by the ITSM lifecycle activities.

- The service portfolio is the collection of services strategically planned for investment and value returns, including present and future services. Think of it as "what you want."

- The service catalog is how the details of services are portrayed and a key item of understanding and communication between the business and the ITSP. Think of it as "how you want it."

- Service levels are the terms and conditions that measure how you get what you want and how you want it. They are the formalization of expectation and delivery between the business and the ITSP.

CHAPTER 4

The IT Service Provider

In the previous chapters, we've built an understanding of what ITSM is, how it benefits the business bottom line, and how to build a profile of business outcomes that can be used to define what you want from the ITSP. Now we will build upon the ITSM foundation by understanding what an ITSP is.

Again, we will use some IT terms for explaining about service providers and its worth noting these because they are helpful to understand the different kinds of providers available in the IT service market today.

Types of ITSP

The beauty of the current state of ITSM maturity is the choice the business customer has to take advantage of. This can actually be an advantage or a disadvantage. Ample choice brings competitive pricing, innovative delivery, and negotiating strength, but to the uneducated consumer, it also leads to mismatched partnerships, missed expectations, and costly mistakes. There are typically three main types of service providers, each with distinct strengths, advantages, and benefits. Most organizations have partnerships with at least two types, and sometimes all three.

Type I ITSP—Internal Customer Dedicated

A type I provider is one that shares the corporate structure with a business unit and often referred to as an internal IT department. The provider mandate is closely tied to the business objectives of the unit, and success is measured in terms of functional performance and cost-effectiveness. Often, the structure of the company has key revenue-generating lines of business as separate departments, and the criticality of the underpinning IT is tied directly to the success and profitability of the line of business. This creates a direct dependency on the ITSP and hence the need for senior corporate control to be direct-line in nature. This often drives the type I provider model to exist for competitive and revenue-generation reasons. Very often, the type I provider operates with a net-zero budget model where it simply recovers or records costs, which are then funded by the business unit in the company. It makes no profit on its own and is often thought of as an expense item on the balance sheet.

The following are distinct characteristics of a type I provider:

- Operates exclusively within an internal market space dictated by the business unit.

- Is tightly coupled with the business unit and managed under a common strategy.

- Decision-making about services is often simplified and quick paced.

- Services are highly customized for the business customer.

- They are generally geared to high service levels.

- Allow the business to avoid certain risks of doing business with third-party providers.

- Service portfolios tend to be smaller and more manageable.

- IT innovation is confined by business growth.

- Will have overlap between ITSPs in common services if no other ITSP type is utilized.

Figure 4-1 depicts a simple structure showing the relationship to the business customer with the type I ITSP.

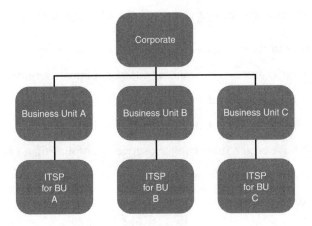

FIGURE 4-1   Type I service provider

Type II ITSP—Internal Shared Services

This type of provider is also an internally focused IT service provider; however, it tends to operate within a shared services structure and offers services to numerous departments or units within the company. This provider generally offers "shared" services, which are corporately used and whose needs are similar across multiple business units.

Examples of shared services are the following:

- **Communication**—Email, phones, desktops, fax

- **Connectivity**—Network, intranet, Internet

- **Support**—Service desk, service catalog

- **Administration**—Human resource systems, financial systems

A type II provider also offers services unique to specific business units as well. The type II provider is governed at the enterprise level and might be funded either at this level entirely, or funded from the enterprise level for shared services and from specific business units for their own services. A type II provider generally will have more complex strategic, tactical, and operational structures for service provision, funding, billing, governance, audit, and so on.

The following are distinct characteristics of a type II provider:

- Ability to share costs and risks across the enterprise
- Can use economies of scale for a larger common-service user base
- Will typically offer market-based pricing
- Can be subject to competition by external providers
- Will have larger, more complex service portfolios than type I
- Geared toward stable one-size-fits-all type of service levels

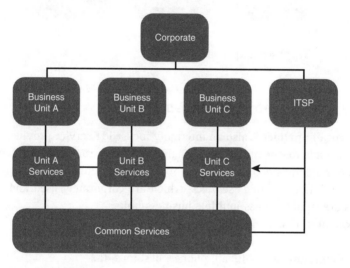

FIGURE 4-2   Type II ITSP

Type III ITSP—External Consolidated

A growing choice among businesses, the type III provider essentially is a third-party provider. There are many styles of service delivery models and descriptive titles for the type III provider, as follows:

- Managed service provider
- Cloud services provider
- Service integrator

- Virtualization service provider

- Agile services provider

The names of type III providers sometimes hold a key to the service model they offer; however, the basic structures are pretty much the same. These providers generally offer bundled ITSM services or specialized services. These are often commoditized, and customers choose from a static array of service types. Price points tend to be competitive, and this type of provider assumes much of the associated overheads and risks, which makes them an attractive provider type. Businesses do not have to invest capital in infrastructures and the associated risks.

Type III providers are business entities and often use a supply chain of types I, II, and III themselves in the execution of services to you as a customer. It is common (although not always effective) for type III providers to be managed by a company's internal type I or II on behalf of the business. In this relationship, the focus of risk and reward is dependent on the business ability to contract and supply-manage the provider effectively. This is an area where ITSM is extremely helpful.

The following are distinct characteristics of a type III provider:

- Independent business with profit model

- Competitive pricing

- Fairly generic or commoditized service models

- Devolved risk and capital investment for business customers

- Less business autonomy

- Business constrained by provider innovation and strategic direction

- Often demand long-term contractual commitment from business customers

- Are often incentivized for performance management

- Can be exploited to meet strategic business goals of outsourcing risk and lowering overall cost of ownership

Figure 4-3 depicts a simple structure for the type III ITSP.

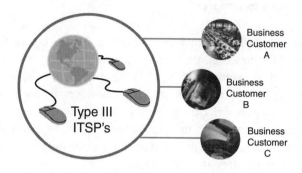

FIGURE 4-3   Type III ITSP

A-ha Moment

Categorizing ITSPs into three basic types makes it easier to see what sets them apart. Most companies will use all three types to some degree and for various services. Try to consolidate the agreements and service catalog items into a single view and insist that your ITSPs all use ITSM frameworks to deliver and manage your services. The business should always remain accountable and ensure that they have an ITSM-knowledge-able resource to coordinate the management of the supply chain.

ITSP Competences

Regardless of the ITSP types you need to fulfill your service needs, each will need to offer specialized resources and capabilities (discussed in the prior chapter) to meet your ITSM demand. What should be a constant in the equation is the competence the ITSP organization has to deliver services.

Within this context, such competences are as follows:

- **Reliable**—The ability to provide what is promised, when it's promised, and how it's promised

- **Experienced**—Can demonstrate a history of providing the type of services you are interested in

- **Proficient**—Can provide information about the management systems and ITSM practices used, which are measurable for efficiency and effectiveness

- **Knowledgeable**—Can prove the workforce engaged in ITSM has the acceptable knowledge to execute

- **Accountable**—Has a documented structure for how accountability is governed and enforced within the parts of the organization that deliver to the customer

- **Skilled**—Can show evidence of the skills of the resources to deliver services

- **Ethical**—Conducts business practices in a responsible manner

- **Trusted**—Can be counted on to preserve an honest, secure and dedicated partnership in the service relationship

- **Accredited**—Possesses the required industry-recognized qualifications both organizationally and individually (more about this later) to do the job

- **Legally compliant**—Meets industry legislated compliance for information technology security

Your ITSPs should meet all competence areas in order to have a harmonious partnership where all parties have similar business philosophies and principles.

ITSP Sourcing

An entire library could be written on this topic. In the ITSM world, sourcing is considered part of the service design model and something every business customer plans well before the service requirements are finalized. There are distinct benefits in doing this because the service itself will take on different characteristics and offer different benefits and costs depending on the sourcing model.

Sourcing is a complex part of the industry, and as new technological innovations emerge, so do new sourcing models. For simplicity sake, we will focus on the various ITSM elements, and three basic sourcing models—insource, outsource, and co-source—and tie these with the ITSP types discussed earlier.

Insourcing

This is a fairly uncomplicated design model that is entirely geared to the type I or II ITSP.

It involves the exclusive use of internal IT service provision, its capabilities, and its resources. The ITSM elements of IT Strategy and Governance are predominantly reserved for internal provision. Compliance, audit, and operational services can also be insourced, but are more commonly an outsourced or co-sourced source model (discussed later in the chapter).

The insourced model typically exists within the organization structures of the company and must have documented service agreements.

TABLE 4-1 Insourcing Advantages and Disadvantages

Advantages	Disadvantages
Direct accountability structures	Business assumes all costs and risks
Freedom of choice	Must maintain a wide base of internal skills and competences
Rapid prototyping of services	Scale limitations
Faster decision-making	Easier tendency to encourage informal process and procedural controls
Company-specific knowledge	Corporate cost constraints can have detrimental impact without the contractual protections
Uniformly governed under corporate structures	
Focused specialization	

Outsourcing

Outsourcing is the use of a type III ITSP and offers a wide array of design model opportunities. Many organizations will use some type of outsourcing, generally for services that the business wants to divest of certain risks and costs. Industry trends can influence design models toward outsourcing, and every business should be aware of the hidden costs and risks that this can produce.

An example of this was the surge of offshoring customer support contact services that gained popularity in the 90's. The driving catalyst was the easy access to cheap labor forces in third-world countries. Many organizations rushed into this model and paid a price for not understanding the importance of all the ITSP competences or lack thereof. Contributing factors in many of these cases were a lack of empowerment for the ITSPs and often understanding of the customer needs, difficulties in communication, overambitious cost cutting leading to unskilled labor, underestimating the true impact of time zone differences, and sometimes an over-reliance on technology. Offshoring can be a perfectly viable, cost-effective choice, and it has evolved significantly in the last decade with many of these factors being addressed.

Another example where industry trends can influence the advantages and disadvantages of sourcing models is technology innovations such as cloud computing. Initially, the technical architectures of cloud computing were costly and reserved for large enterprise customers and ITSPs, but as the economies of scale have evolved, this trend as an example has become affordable as a service design model for any size ITSP and customer. Changes in industry trends such as these have made outsourcing effective and affordable and widened the scope for what type of services can be outsourced.

TABLE 4-2   Outsourcing Advantages and Disadvantages

Advantages	Disadvantages
Business divests some costs and risks	Indirect accountability structures
Economies of scale	Requires supplier management effort
Can be transient or longer-term acquisition	Less customization opportunity
Can be focused on specific services or entire portfolio	Less direct control
Lower overall cost of ownership	Exit complexity
Competitive market	Integration challenges
Time to market speed	Dependent on supplier solvency
Less human resource overhead management	More complex supply chain
Somewhat shielded from rapid cost-cutting initiatives	
Access to current technologies and innovations with less overhead to monitor these trends	

Co-Sourcing

An increasingly popular and commonly available model, this hybrid model comes in a variety of shapes and sizes. At a basic level, it should be considered a shared risk and reward-based model. All ITSP types can participate in this, and as such, it offers the highest level of flexibility to meet a business's service needs. Highly flexible can also mean highly complex, so care is needed to determine whether this is a viable model for your needs.

Typically, co-sourcing involves the cooperation of a number of ITSPs in the provision of service either for individual services or a group of them. In this model, clarification of the roles and responsibilities of each ITSP and the business is crucial to avoid unnecessary overlap, duplication, or gaps in service coverage and management.

One of the strongest advantages is the ability to integrate all ITSM elements and services together into a comprehensive program. It affords the safety of internal controls with the divestment and sharing of risk and reward.

TABLE 4-3   Co-sourcing Advantages and Disadvantages

Advantages	Disadvantages
Business divests some costs and risks	Indirect accountability structures
Largest economy of scale	Requires highly developed supplier management skills
Affords shared services across multiple businesses	Lowest customization opportunity
Potential for the lowest possible cost of ownership	Lowest level of direct control
Generally longer-term committed partnerships	Highly complex
Competitive market	Integration challenges
Time to market speed	Dependent on inter-supplier cooperation
Highly flexible service	Complex service management process management
Ability to exploit innovation and asset use for harmony value provision across a large supply chain	Requires attention to ensure cultural and acceptance
Wide choice of suppliers	Higher security and legislated compliance
Allows businesses to take advantage of cutting-edge service models and technologies	

What Should Influence Your Sourcing Decisions?

As a business, you should carefully consider what things should influence sourcing decisions. There are no hard and fast rules about this, but there are some questions you should consider to help you decide the best route, as follows:

1. **Are you able to maintain all the skills and experience reliably internally for all your service needs?**

   Consider that there is a significant cost associated to this, not to mention risks.

2. **Does your business strategy typically include rapid growth?**

   The costs of supporting services will also increase, and type II and III providers can often offer the best economies of scale in this type of situation.

3. **Does your business offer new products and services to your customers on a regular basis?**

   There will undoubtedly be additional IT services needed to support new business products and services, so in this situation, the business cycle from an ITSM perspective is rapidly changing. Time to market speed of the supporting IT services and service management capabilities will be a key factor in sustaining high-quality business services, so take this into account when selecting a sourcing model and suppliers.

4. **What is the corporate appetite for risk and investment in IT?**

   You must understand the core business and the philosophy for risk and investment when deciding on sourcing models. Because type III can offer the highest cost and risk avoidance, it might be considered the best choice, but be clear on the tradeoffs that come with that, such as less flexibility and control (refer to ITSP type II advantage and disadvantages).

5. **Does your business have the capability to manage a supply chain effectively?**

   Do not underestimate the effort involved in this. A business should be prepared to dedicate resources to supplier management and have requisite ITSM experience at a senior level to ensure ITSM integration in the delivery and support of your services. This is not an insurmountable task, but one that is often neglected until trouble arises.

6. **Does the direction of your business often involve innovation and cutting-edge products and services?**

   The reliance on similar innovative capabilities from IT and ITSM will likely be the difference between success and failure on the business side of this equation. Choose the ITSP who can demonstrate the capacity to stay current and lead innovation in IT.

7. **Does your business tend to have the support and participation of its senior management?**

   Moving toward a comprehensive ITSM program, and ITSPs capable of delivering services in this way, requires an amount of cultural change. Process-based service provision requires a service-focused set of attitudes, behaviors, and culture that might not already be present in your company. Management has to be engaged, committed, and in it for the long term.

Sourcing models of any kind require ITSM to be successful. Even though it is considered best practice, it does require commitment, resources, and cultural change, so be sure to consider your business's appetite for committing these things when choosing the kinds of service partnerships you can sustain. Remember that your ITSPs are only a part of the success story—you are the other part.

Companies who have made the commitments are the ones who enjoy the most beneficial, risk-tolerant, and profitable organizations in the world. In the next chapter, we'll move on to ITSP negotiation!

CHAPTER 5

The Negotiation

So far, we have explored what ITSM is all about, what a service is, how you articulate your needs, and the various types of service providers there are. After the sourcing model is selected, the next step is to negotiate the terms of service. There are a few ways in which this is likely to occur:

- **Formal tendering**—If a formal acquisition such as a tender is required, the negotiation can occur as part of the documented requirements and evaluation of bid responses or a supplier chosen and terms negotiated as part of the formal contract.

- **Integrator**—If a multiple supplier model is chosen, you might have an integrator whose role it is to coordinate the provision of service to you from across the supply chain. The negotiation of terms and conditions will often be through the integrator that you have selected and empowered with specific delegated authorities on your behalf.

- **Sole source**—If a formal competitive process is not used (that is, a tender), or only a single supplier meets your needs, negotiation will occur as part of establishing the contract.

- **Internal sourcing**—If you use an internal IT department, you might need to negotiate the terms of a new service being introduced, renegotiate existing terms as the result of contract expiration, identified improvements, or as the result of a regularly scheduled review.

The advice here is applicable whether you are negotiating with an internal IT department within your own company or business unit, or outsourced ITSPs. Where there are unique specifics, they will be added.

Negotiation is essential, not optional. The purpose is to establish your expectations and needs and how these are to be provided. This sets the tone for the quality you expect and failing to negotiate is a clear sign that you don't care about quality. If you leave the impression that quality is not important, the ITSP will expect you not to measure it afterward.

Decision Styles

Negotiation is activity and decisions are the output. In many organizations, there are established ways and means by which decisions are made. This may also apply to ITSP negotiations. Make sure that you understand the implications of how decisions are made in your organization before you set out to commit your company to an agreement with an ITSP. The following sections briefly describe some common decision styles.

Policy-Driven

For some companies, sourcing decisions are driven at the organization's governance level. Sourcing policies might already be in place and are intended to set boundaries or simply guidance to direct the selection of suppliers that can conform to a certain organizational standard.

The standards can include

- The type of relationship the supplier must have within the supply chain

- The technology architecture or platforms that must be used

- The financial model of the relationship that will be used

- Perhaps whether the organization's IT needs should be filled internally, externally, or a blend of both

Corporately shared services are a good example of ones that might be policy-driven. These services are used across the company, so it makes sense to require a standard be used. This can minimize cost to own, operate, and support. ITSM refers to this as "total cost of ownership" or TCO. So, the governance body might have established that corporate services must run on company standard desktops, laptops, and mobile devices and accessed through a virtual private network.

This tells us a few things already about what terms and conditions we need from the ITSP who will provide and support email. It might also tell us what sourcing models are appropriate for acquiring the service. We still, however, must negotiate the specifics of how the service is provided and supported.

Figure 5-1 follows a flow of policy-driven sourcing.

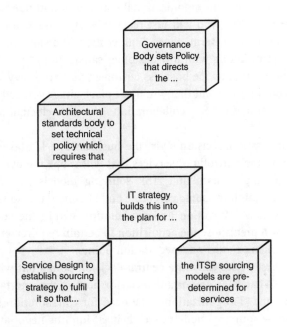

FIGURE 5-1   Policy-driven sourcing

Collaboration-Driven

Many companies are becoming innovative in collaborating for sourcing, negotiation, and ITSP management. This helps ensure awareness across the organization of emerging needs, among business units, balancing cost, quality, and acquisition in a coordinated manner and avoiding duplication, conflicting expectations, and costly mistakes. It also gives the business something extremely valuable: leverage.

A central collaboration point can be a group of stakeholders who informally meet and agree upon sourcing strategy, future requirements (because we want to be proactive), and the balance of the supply chain (who does what and when). It can also be a top-down driven situation where policy is handed down from a governance body that is used by a stakeholder group to commence sourcing activity.

ITSPs who have experience providing service to multiple business units will often make it a requirement to have a central point of interface so that needs are vetted from an organizational standpoint and not an individual view. There are ITSPs who will just react to every request and charge for that, but over the long-term, chaos, high costs, and disjointed service provision will result (along with low customer satisfaction).

It's important that as the business customer, you are savvy with respect to central coordination and that you don't place either yourself or the ITSP in a no-win situation. So, collaboration is a key element in sourcing decisions.

In a collaboration decision style, the business and IT stakeholders will collaborate on the portfolio of services that will shape the overall requirements for a supply chain and ITSP sourcing models (see Figure 5-2). Although there might be some corporate and IT constraints to work within, this model values innovation and exploitation within the supply chain. These facts will predispose the acquisition to certain requirements and help drive the sourcing model and negotiation points.

Both of these styles illustrate central decision points but with different approaches. What is an important facet for both is the interface between the business and IT organizations. The need for collaboration in selecting the appropriate sourcing models extends itself into the negotiation process and the relationship that is born when the agreement is signed.

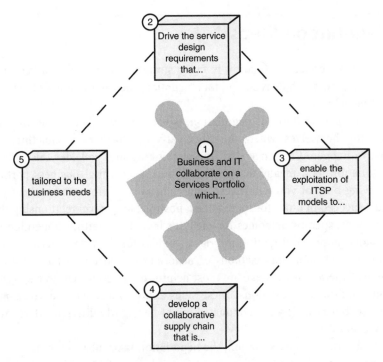

FIGURE 5-2   Collaboration decision style

A-ha Moment

The presence of collaboration from the beginning of this process helps deal with the elements of the relationship that are not always easy to document as "terms and conditions" within the contract itself. Collaboration allows each party in the relationship to have input, to see all sides of the issue or opportunity, and to build trust. There are differences in the negotiation points needed based on the nature of the services themselves. This adds to the building of mutual experience which inevitably makes things run smoother.

There are numerous models for IT service provision, and in the previous chapter, we looked at a few basic ones. What is constant in these models is the need to negotiate the full range of service elements.

Negotiation Steps

The art of service negotiation is fairly straightforward. First, agree upon the overarching objectives, and then negotiate the finer points of how they will be achieved.

Some people think of negotiation as each party trying to get the best deal for themselves, where the other party has to give up something for that to happen. Challenge that line of thinking and consider this type of negotiation as a means to collaborate with a potential business partner, knowing both of you will invest time, money, and effort, and both of you must succeed in order for there to be a positive, long-term relationship that creates prosperous outcomes for each. It's less about getting something for less and more about getting the right services for the right price.

There are numerous methods of negotiation, and here I have distilled some of them that I believe are most helpful to IT service contracts, terms, and conditions negotiations. These steps apply to any method you might choose, but how they are conducted might be slightly different. Here are a few examples.

In a formal tender situation, the negotiation takes place more indirectly at first. The consumer will state their needs as established requirements within the tender documentation. Potential suppliers will respond to the tender with their plan to meet your requirements, and they will often reciprocate with some requirements of your business in order to fulfill the service. This is a form of negotiation. You will weigh each supplier response, and you might exchange further detail, including a presentation or discussion with potential suppliers before making a final decision. After a decision is reached, the contract is based largely on the points negotiated during the tender evaluation process.

When you are acquiring a large number of services, and this will be delivered using numerous suppliers, often companies will opt to use an integrator, whose role is to coordinate everything from the negotiation of terms and conditions and the delivery of services over the life of the contract. The integrator will be an IT specialist organization who understand what your needs are and how they are likely to be best met within a chain of supply. An integrator will often be at the center of negotiation and will use their position of knowledge to ensure that the contract will meet expectations. The integrator will also serve as the escalation point for both business and the ITSP.

Sole sourcing is used for smaller service acquisition or when the requirements and constraints are so specialized that only a single provider can offer them or is willing to. This involves direct negotiation between the consumer and the provider.

Internal sourcing is like sole sourcing in that you are dealing with one organization, which happens to be within your own company. Negotiation will be direct and usually between two senior-level executives or designates. This type of negotiation can become emotionally charged, negatively competitive, or, worse, too casual and not well documented. Often, this situation, although it might seem to be the easiest, can actually produce the worst results due to the types of situations described here. Some companies will hire the services of an expert to broker the negotiations in an impartial and neutral manner.

Regardless of the type, all negotiations should include the following basic steps:

1. Agree upon main high-level objectives of each party.

2. Establish a main service contract with overarching terms and definitions.

3. Establish service agreements for core and specialty services:

   a. With detailed terms of service.

   b. Service monitoring and reporting terms.

   c. Measures for performance, function, and operational norms.

   d. Continuity and security assurance.

   e. Service review points, change, and improvement triggers and actions.

Each step forms deeper elements of the overall contract between the parties, as shown in the illustration of Figure 5-3.

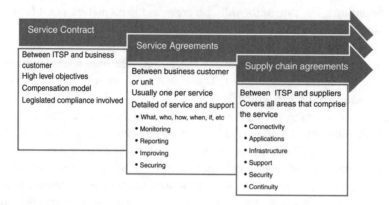

FIGURE 5-3   Negotiated agreements for a service

A-ha Moment

In order to gain the most advantage from ITSM, we must dispel the notion that the point of negotiating service agreements is to get "more for less." ITSM is really more about getting "right for right"—the right service for the right price. Superior service quality and performance contributes to your business bottom line and is about a partnership of service management philosophy, where value creation for each partner creates profit and a win/win situation for both.

Agree Upon the Objectives

Remember the lesson about business outcome statements from Chapter 2, "ITSM: The Business Asset"? It's that level of granularity we are aiming for here. The objectives should be high-level, succinct, and meaningful within the context of the agreements that will underpin them. They can be documented as terms of reference for the service provision and signed off by the accountable representatives from the business and the ITSP.

The Business View

You need two things from the ITSP: the service and support for it. You want some basic assurances from each thing.

Service assurance:

- The service will do what it's supposed to.

- The service will meet the functional and performance requirements asked for.

- The service will achieve the business outcomes asked for.

Support assurance:

- The supplier will fully support the service according to what was requested.

- The supplier will respond to issues as agreed.

- The supplier will make sure the service is secure and operating optimally at all times as agreed (keeps on doing what it's supposed to).

The Supplier View

To provide the service and support the business wants, it has to play a role in making that possible.

Service assurance:

- The customer has accurately stated its requirements.

- The customer accepts that changes beyond those initially agreed upon will cost extra.

- The customer commits the time, resources, and knowledge needed.

Support assurance:
- The customer fully understands the service levels it is paying for.

- The customer will request support for the service in the agreed-upon manner every time.

- The customer will provide advanced notice of potential and planned significant changes in demand.

The business and the ITSP should create basic statements for these objectives, which then become the basis for negotiations and the contracts and agreements needed to support the service(s).

A-ha Moment

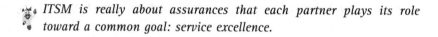 *ITSM is really about assurances that each partner plays its role toward a common goal: service excellence.*

The Service Contract

The service contract is a document that outlines these basic services and sets them within some usually legally binding terms. This protects both parties by establishing the scope of the relationship and what the relationship will produce over the term of the contract. The following sections are a good starting point.

Parties

The service contract should clearly indicate whom the contract is between. This should include the legal company entity information, but also the department, unit, or area, as it would normally be referred to.

Term

Every service contract must include a start and end period within which the terms and conditions apply. Special attention should be paid here to carefully documenting the period of advance notice either party must provide before terminating the contract, allowing it to expire, or making changes to the terms or conditions. It should also contain any terms relating to optional extensions or renewals of the contract with or without re-negotiation of particular clauses.

Services Covered

Generally, a service contract will cover multiple services and possibly multiple business units. These should be listed specifically to avoid any confusion over scope and who is a part of the contract and who is not. This is extremely important where a company's IT department is negotiating service provision on behalf of all or parts of the business.

Business Units Covered

The contract should stipulate which parts of the company are covered under the service contract. In many cases a contract might be specific to a single business unit and to avoid confusion, this should be clearly identified.

Service Agreements Covered

The creation of the service agreement will be covered in detail in the next chapter, but all service agreements which fall under the terms of the governing contract must be listed. This can be shown as an appendix and added later on. The list of service agreements should be reviewed regularly and review reminders built into the Change Management process so that the list of agreements is kept up to date.

Contacts

This should cover specifics about who can sign on behalf of each party listed in the contract, who will actively manage the contract, who can authorize changes to it, and who the business, IT, and provider contacts are for each of these areas. This could be a person, but perhaps also the role to assure continuity in the event of personnel changes.

Changes

This is a critical part of the contract and should cover who can request, authorize, and fulfill changes to the contract, how this will be done, and how notification to all parties shown in the "parties" and "role" sections will occur.

Reports

The contract should specify the types of reports, frequency, and basic content that each party expects to receive as a result of the contract arrangement. This should not be confused with service performance reports, which will be covered later. The reports are related to activities that relate to the service contract, such as changes to the terms, roles, contact information or additional services added to the contract.

Financial Records

The contract should stipulate the nature and types of financial records each party needs to have access to during the term of the contract. This will include when either party will inspect the financial records, the period of retention, security of the information, and other pertinent information required either under law or through corporate policy.

Confidentiality

This clause should be specific about the need for protection of sensitive information for both parties and how this must be safeguarded by each partner. There will often be additional legislative compliance to information privacy and protection that may be referenced here for completeness. This is also a good clause to add any freedom of information law that affects access to information for the contract or information generated as a result of the contract.

Indemnity

This is common in most countries to have each partner indemnify the other with certain restrictions on liability. This will vary by state, region, or country and often within corporate sectors as well.

Dispute Resolution

Despite best attempts, there might be concerns, complaints, issues, and disputes that arise over specifics of the service provision. This can occur from any of the parties to the contract. Ensuring that disputes are handled effectively is important BEFORE they occur. This section should include any

imes the business customer and the ITSP are not located in the
ntry. In these instances it's often customary to use the governing
e country where the business customer is established as a legal
ne rule, generally speaking, is the company who issues (lets) the
is the one whose governing laws presides.
the service contract is agreed and signed off, the next step is likely
e most important documentation within the partnership; The ser-
ements. These agreements set out the details about service deliv-
these will be judged, by whom, and what the customers can
n terms of service quality and management.
ill cover this in Chapter 6, "The Service Agreement."

escalating procedures, who needs to be inv
makes the ultimate decisions for disputes. 1
ble resolution through consensus building,
tion, but both need to be included and the :

Financial Compensation

This describes the charging model and any i
plier and service performance. This should c
any periodic or anomalous charges. The ap
should also be described.

Legislative Compliance

This is an important area to cover within tl
identify any compliance-related areas that ea
to. Some common ones are reporting, info
workplace safety, environmental, and other ge

Definitions

To ensure a common understanding of wha
(especially those that describe a service), a l
included. Remember that the service contract i
can cover numerous services with the same I1
do so. Although there is nothing wrong with
for each service (and this might be manda
providers for each service), it does add extra a

Appendix B is an example of a service cont

Contracts of any type may also need to c
indicate the governing law of the state, region,
may also require specific clauses to conform
standards within your company's industry sect
covered all of these areas as well as the on
arrangements.

Due to the diversity of business needs, corpo
dards, and so on, there is no single way to comp
tract for every situation. The previous informati
and be accompanied with guidance by your loc
try legislation, and legal opinion.

Som
same c
law of
entity.
contrac

Once
to beco
vice ag
ery, ho
expect

We

CHAPTER 6

The Service Agreement

Sometimes called service level agreements, these document the particulars of each service. In terms of the ongoing management of services and measuring against customer expectations, service agreements form the baseline on which quality is measured and success or failure established. **This is where a savvy business customer can negotiate meaningful terms that significantly impact the business bottom line.**

Each service agreement will be slightly different in what it contains, based on the service details, but every service agreement should contain a minimum list of detailed information (each of these are negotiation points). First, we will look at the basic content areas for a service agreement and examples of what you should consider covering during the negotiation of a service agreement.

Before we get to that part, it's worth mentioning that service agreements are not just documented checklists. They are living agreements that should reflect the recognition of unique situations, local knowledge, empowerment, and judgment, and they require managers to manage, not just wave the document around when something goes wrong. They are the guiding tenets of what both parties are trying to achieve with the service partnership, and the tools that provide the ability to deliver this, measure this, manage this, and improve this.

Appendix C will illustrate an example of a service agreement.

Because a service agreement is intended to contain specific details about a service, try to avoid a common mistake: grouping too many disparate services under one agreement. It's hard to reach the correct level of granularity when trying to document service needs of both apples and oranges! The industry offers some guidance about what types of service agreements to consider using and these are worth noting here. I've adapted some of these for you to think about how they might work for your needs.

Core Service Agreements

Earlier, we defined core services as being a service with basic elements, likely to be used by a number of business units—things like email or telephony as an example. Core services will be subject to specific terms of operation that could apply to numerous customers. This type of service agreement can also be appended with the next type: the service package agreement that is for enhanced features of a core service that customers might want for unique or upgraded service needs. An example of this might be extra email storage capacity or enhanced user support for specific user needs. As a generic type of agreement, these would align to a single service used by one or more customers. ITIL best practice refers to this as a service-based service level agreement.

Service Package Agreements

These types of service agreements are useful for grouping similar types of services that business areas need. Here, the agreements can be for enhanced core services, or for grouped services. In this case, the service agreements are more specific than core service agreements and will often have pricing options for varying levels of services. Example of service package agreements could be financial services, which could cover basic business financial applications plus monthly report production and be accessible to specific users within a business unit as part of overall services that are available to multiple business units. This type of agreement is usually developed for a specific customer and ITIL refers to this as a customer-based SLA.

These two basic service agreement structures can be used in a variety of formats and adapted for use with many different services and customers.

Whichever types of service agreements you choose to use, either the ones described here or something created by your company, there are some basic elements that should be contained within any type of service agreement.

Service Description

This should be a simple and straightforward description of what the service is. Think back to outcome statements. They are useful for this purpose and can be used as the start point for creating the service description.

Example: Email: Company employees can receive, create, and store electronic messages on desktops and mobile devices.

General negotiation points include the following:

- You and the ITSP must agree that the description of the service adequately portrays it.

- You should require that the ITSP use this service description consistently in places such as the service catalog, service reports, and automated service management tools.

Service Hours

This should describe when the business expects the service to be available for use (for example, 8:00 am to 5:00 pm, 7 x 24 x 365, Monday to Friday, or whatever the business has deemed as the requirement). *(Note: There is a direct relationship between availability levels and cost. Higher means higher!)*

Service hours should reflect the accurate usage needs for your business users. It's nice to think that every service could be available all the time, any time we happen to need it, but service hours like this are prohibitively expensive. Chances are that most services will be available just about all the time. (Service providers do not generally shut them off outside of service hours except for maintenance.)

What you are really stating here is the availability that you are willing to pay for and that the ITSP will be measured against in terms of their performance in accordance with the service contract and agreement.

General negotiation points include the following:

- For most companies, there are core hours where the service is heavily used. It might be available 24 hours a day, but there will be trends in demand that you should understand. Make the service hours and support hours coincide with the demand peak times and lessen the need for a high level of support response during low usage times. **You can save a lot of money by simply understanding your usage trends and using that as a base for agreeing what service hours need to be.**

There may also be a need to have additional caveats to the core service hours for special circumstances such as public holidays, business cycles, or ad-hoc needs. These should be stated in addition to core service hours.

- So, think about your true service availability needs and base negotiation on this. Some questions to answer that might help you figure out your availability are the following:

  1. Do the majority of your users work on weekends?

  2. Do you have shift workers using the service around the clock, or are there core business hours?

  3. Does this service enable a critical business process that would cause harm to your business profits, reputation, or health and safety if it were not available when you needed it?

  4. Are there company or public holidays when most of the workforce is not using these services?

  5. Are there periods in your business cycle where this service is critical, such as the end of the month, reporting periods, sales cycles, and so on?

  Use these and other questions relevant to your situation and to the service in question to formulate some trend intelligence to base your service availability demands of the ITSP on.

- The ITSP generally will offer better pricing for predictable patterns of consumption and user behaviors. If you can provide fairly predictable usage patterns, you should demand the best prices. Expect to pay premium prices for unpredictable usage. The ITSP has to live up to the service agreement terms and will err on the side of caution to do so, and this will require additional and often costly infrastructure that may sit idle and only for insurance to meet your demands.

A-ha Moment

Business consumption of services is referred to as service capacity. Capacity is a major cost factor in how much a service costs. The ITSP passes these on to the customer. Taking time to understand how you currently use a service can provide insight into how to predict capacity needs for a new service or an existing one subjected to some business growth or downsizing plans. Trending service usage can ensure that you don't overpay for service from your ITSP or, worse, underestimate needs and experience disruption. To put this into a business context, think about what you already know about how you meet your customer's demands for your products or services. There tends to be a correlation to those and your service needs. That's a good place to start thinking about capacity.

Customer Support

This is an area that is often not properly negotiated, and many dysfunctional contracts are the result of improperly understood positions of either party around support.

There are some basic areas that you should consider covering in the negotiation stage to ensure that you understand the costs, implications, and what you can expect related to support. Most business customers equate how well a service is supported as a measure of how good the ITSP is. Many ITSP suffer complaints and accusations of poor quality when in fact they are delivering exactly the level of support paid for. This is no consolation, however, for either party, and does nothing to quell the perceptional issues. The best course of action is to negotiate this properly in the first place, and then ensure that ALL users understand what is being paid for.

Some of the basics that should always be covered in customer support are the ITSP management of the following:

- Incidents
- Problems
- Changes

- Reporting

- Complaints

- Reviews

Next, we'll look at some specific areas to consider in negotiation based on how an ITSP manages your services.

Management of Incidents

When the customer experiences an unexpected disruption in service quality or availability, a clear mechanism for support should be understood. There are specific activities an ITSP will use to manage an incident, as shown in Figure 6-1.

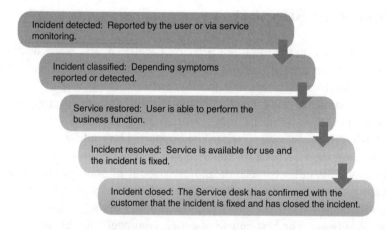

FIGURE 6-1   Incident management flow

Incident Management Negotiation Points

- **Detection:** The ITSP should use system monitoring to detect events that can be fixed before an incident occurs. Determine whether the ITSP does this and what the event thresholds are. Beyond event detection, you should negotiate the agreed time elapse between the time an incident is reported and when work on it begins. So, you will want to include the following:

- Time to answer the call to the service desk

- Time that work commences on the incident

- **Classification:** The ITSP should use a classification system for incidents to your service that indicate its priority (to YOU as the business customer). This is calculated using a table of values you should provide, which are as follows:

  - *Impact:* The impact this type of incident has on your business at the time it is experienced (that is, how many people are affected).

  - *Urgency:* How quickly the incident must be resolved before greater impact is experienced (that is, high urgency means faster time to fix).

  - A sample priority table is shown in Figure 6-2.

		Impact		
		High	Medium	Low
	High	1	2	3
Urgency	Medium	2	3	4
	Low	3	4	5

Priority level	Description	Target Resolution
1	Critical	30 minutes
2	High	2 hours
3	Medium	24 hours
4	Low	48 hours
5	Planned activity	As planned

FIGURE 6-2   Example of impact, urgency, and priority scale

- You and the ITSP should commit to a classification system for service incidents (that might look something like Figure 6-2). It drives quality measures and determines the level of effort and cost to support your service. Pricing will also apply according to the level of priority because it will cost more to respond faster and fix faster.

- **Restored:** This is the time elapsed between classification and the service being restored. Note: Restored means that you can once again carry out the business process, not necessarily that the incident is resolved. The ITSP may provide a temporary workaround for you to get back to business while the ITSP continues to work on the incident.

- **Resolved:** This is when the incident is fixed. The time elapsed between restoration and resolution is often a point of negotiation and certainly is of quality measurement. You want assurance that temporary fixes are not the rule, but the exception!

- **Closed:** Make sure the closure of the incident is ONLY after the customer agrees it has been fixed and not when the ITSP thinks service is restored. This is an important point to negotiate because it affects the perception of quality and allows the customer to confirm that the service is working properly.

Management of Problems

In ITSM, a problem has a special meaning. It is the process used to find the cause of recurring incidents or issues that need to be identified and fixing them permanently. From a business perspective, there is a major interest in making sure your ITSP does this because it saves money, time, disruption to business services, and allows proactive management of your service to occur. On a day-to-day basis, you won't normally be involved directly with problem management but you should be sure that your ITSP is.

Lots of business customers fail to understand the significance of investing in problem management capability for the support of their services, but countless dollars are kept within the business bottom line when this is done effectively.

The problem lifecycle begins when, through either system monitoring or users reporting incidents, a recurring theme is revealed. Something of unknown cause is creating a service disruption, often repeatedly.

Problem Management Negotiation Points

You want to be certain your ITSP is capable of conducting problem management. So, be sure it can do the following:

- Trend incidents and identify possible problems
- Identify root causes and rectify them

- Report on impact of problem management to a reduction in incidents

- Report on the overall increase in service availability from problem management

Change Management

Every service will undergo changes. Some of these are planned as part of business growth and some for technical maintenance and improvements. Every year, businesses lose millions of dollars when unplanned, or poorly managed, changes are introduced that create incidents. In fact, change-related failure is the number-one cause of service disruptions. This makes change management a critical negotiation point in a service agreement.

Change Management Negotiation Points

The idea here is to ensure that as part of your service agreement, there is a clear understanding of when, who, and how changes are undertaken. Every change should follow an established process that includes the basics, shown in Figure 6-3.

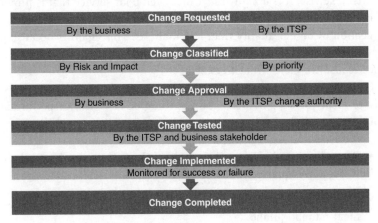

FIGURE 6-3   Change management basic flow

In terms of negotiation, you should discuss and agree upon:

- Who can authorize any change to a service

- Who can request a change to a service

- When changes are made (usually prescheduled and communicated)

- That every high risk or critical service change has a back-out plan in the event that it fails, which restores business service quickly

- That every change is ranked by risk to the business

- Every high-risk change is discussed with the business prior to a decision to implement it

- That the business has input to change approvals

- That changes are tested before they are implemented except in emergency situations

Service Reporting

The fastest way to erode a perfectly good business/ITSP relationship is to let perception be the measure of success. There is a saying within the ITSM industry that even if an ITSP provides a reliable service 99.99% of the time, it will be remembered and judged by the .01% it didn't. This is because we allow perception to cloud the truth of how good or bad the ITSP is. Likewise, it is a known fact that even poor service that is provided consistently, in the same way to the customer every time, will leave the perception of higher quality than it actually is! This again is because perception can easily fool us into thinking something is good when it isn't just because we know what to expect.

Each of these scenarios has a hidden cost to the business. The easiest way to dispel or support perception is to agree how service performance will be reported. At a minimum, you want to negotiate the following:

- Reports at regular interval that measure predetermined periods (that is, monthly, quarterly, and so on).

- The information must be relevant to the business, not full of technical mumbo jumbo.

- The information must be set against a backdrop that makes it relevant (that is, compared to the last period, peer norms, agreed targets, or the service agreement).

- Should paint an immediate picture of quality levels.

- Should explain any discrepancies.

- Should provide remedial information.

- Should provide targets for next period.

- Who will review the information with the business.

- Who from the business will review the report with the ITSP.

- What incentives are forthcoming for exceeding the targets—this is for both business and ITSP because both have a role to play.

- That exceeding targets provides tangible business value, not just speed. You might not want or need to pay for speed!

- What penalties are forthcoming for not meeting the targets—this also is for both business and IT because both can be the cause of targets not being met.

- That the report provides a basis for positive discussion, not a finger-pointing exercise.

- That the report forms the basis for improvements for the next period.

Service Complaints

Customer satisfaction is at the center of all productive business/IT relationships. It's not enough to just measure customer satisfaction by periodic surveys alone. The ITSP must provide a well-functioning mechanism for dealing with service complaints. What is also true is that if the business is playing its role responsibly in the service relationship, it will be involved in establishing a high level of awareness among its users about the service agreement, its terms, its conditions, and the role the users must play to also support good service quality. ITSP satisfaction also needs to be part of the equation and ITSP complaints need to be factored into how service complaints are handled. If customers are not fulfilling their part in the service partnership, the ITSP should have the means to discuss and agree a solution.

Complaints should not be regarded as the avenue for customer whining. To be worth the effort, they have to be regarded as a symptom of something not working, an opportunity to be proactive in improving the relationship or service, and that the ITSP can have legitimate complaints as well for the same purpose. During negotiation, ensure that the following points are agreed upon:

- How complaints are documented: form, style, and content.

- Who receives them on behalf of the ITSP and the business.

- How they are classified for investigation.

- Who is involved in investigating them.

- How long a response will take (you might want to use a similar table for impact, urgency, and priority here).

- How complaints feed into the service review (to be covered next).

Service Reviews

Reports, surveys, complaints, and measurement agreements are all important facets of good service management. They mean little, however, if nothing is done with them that rectifies a deficiency, improves quality, or levels praise for excellent performance. Service reviews are intended to create actions from the retrospective views gained over a period of time.

Ask any customer who takes the time to participate in a survey, fills out a suggestion or complaint form, and then never hears anything beyond that, how often they will continue to do so.

A service review is often the completion of a cycle within the service agreement. It marks a commitment by each party in the agreement to do more than pay lip service to the agreement and actually create actions to improve quality.

Service reviews should be built into the service agreement through negotiation of the form, style, frequency, and participation of players in the review. Each subsequent review period should evaluate progress from agreed action of the prior period. You should negotiate these particulars and agree upon the commencing review time and ongoing duration. The participants should be individuals that represent all stakeholder areas, be knowledgeable, and have authority to recommend and delegate improvement activities. Just having service review meetings will not do the trick— they must be acted upon, followed up, managed, and completed for there to be any forward momentum for improvement or innovation. Businesses and ITSPs often miss this as an opportunity to create innovation for improvement as well. They often view the review meeting as a means to discuss shortcomings, and although this is often true, there should also be time set aside for discussing innovation ideas that might either address an issue or take the service quality to the next level of maturity.

A-ha Moment

The art of negotiating service agreements comprises a large part of how good the service quality experience will be. To many companies, this is what service management IS about. Regardless of the type of ITSP or service model you use, negotiation points remain basically the same. If your ITSP is your internal IT department or a cloud computing vendor, what you need in an agreement is relatively the same. You need assurance that you get the kind of service you need, when you need it, for the right price, and confidence that service quality is planned for and not just a lucky event.

Similar to service contracts, there is no single set of elements that is right or wrong. The ones previously described are some basic tried and true elements. Ensure you adapt and create the complete list that meets your partnership needs.

In the next chapter, we will tie this altogether and look at how this partnership looks in action in a variety of service models.

CHAPTER 7

The Partnership in Action

Throughout this book, I have emphasized a genuine importance of the partnership between the business and its ITSPs as the prime ingredient for success. In this chapter, we'll look at how a successful partnership works, how to measure the signs of ITSM quality, and overall health and improvements.

The importance of the key messages in the prior chapter—that there must be agreement on what will be done, who will do it, and how success will be measured—takes on critical meaning here. Once the partnership goes into action, a failure to have done this beforehand makes it impossible to quickly agree on process, procedure and responsibility when things are in the midst of going wrong.

While we have already discussed the ingredients that make the ITSM partnership work, every partnership is dynamic; sometimes it's easy to get out of balance or lose focus, and the only thing that makes us realize we are out of balance is a problem. That's too late, and there's a lot we can do to avoid finding ourselves that far down a bumpy road.

The Partner Compass

The success of the ITSM partnership is influenced by the *partner compass*. This compass is our gauge of direction, course correction, and achieving the objective of proper balance that remains on a steady, productive course. The idea of the partner compass comes from the adaptation of an old business concept that many companies (for example, Disney) have used as their quality experience gauge for the theme park experience and how they provide customer service. The compass concept helps keep competing tensions of service delivery, perceptions, and needs balanced to maximize service quality.

The partner compass sets four main balance points, as follows:

- Needs—The clarity and acceptance of the needs of each partner. If the business needs overpower the ITSP's abilities, they will not be met. If the ITSP needs are not taken into account by the business, service quality may suffer. Needs will vary in their intensity over the lifecycle of the service and may shift on a daily, weekly, monthly, or other periodic cycle. Keeping needs in balance requires each party to be aware of the needs of the other at all times, and to do this requires communication. A few rules of guidance are worth remembering:

  - **Needs do change.** Most should be anticipated, but not all can be. Be prepared to have occasional hiccups when needs arise that cannot have been anticipated. The success is in knowing how to adapt and adjust to them without creating undue disadvantage on either side of the partnership.

  - **Consistency creates comfort.** Even though we cannot always achieve 100% satisfaction, being consistent in how we meet needs creates a sense of security that even if there are some misses, our providers' eyes are ever watchful and looking out for our needs. Consistency involves both giving and receiving service. Good customers are as important to success as good service providers are.

  - **Needs require active management to reinforce realistic, measured, and proven value and accuracy.** Assuming that either party instinctively has realistic views of their needs at all times, especially in dynamically changing businesses, will bring the partner compass out of balance quickly. Active points of reference for gauging and assessing needs at specific trigger points should be agreed within the partnership.

  - **Understand the difference between a "need" and a "want."** Accept that wants are the bonus when we get something we should not expect. Needs are today, and wants are sometimes tomorrow's improvement opportunity or an intended direction in the future.

- Wants—These are opportunities to add to the service experience either for the customer or the ITSP. Generally, wants will fall into two basic categories: One comes about when, during the regular course of service provision or consumption, an idea is formed for enhancing or improving a service, how it's delivered, or how it's consumed. These are experiential and come from either the customer's experience with using a service and how it can be improved, or from the provider's experience in delivering it and how this could be improved. Sometimes, the "want" is something that is directly related to a particular service; the process or the "want" is actually an idea for a new service or technology for process enhancement. Wants can also come about for the wrong reasons—unmanaged expectations for service boundaries and what is possible within the agreed contract and failure to actively manage wants when business needs change.

- Emotions—The people working within the partnership will have emotions with respect to the partnership experiences. Every interaction between the partners will result in a positive, negative, or neutral type of emotion. These tend to color our perception of needs, wants, and stereotypes. Emotions are constant in the relationship and tend to swing between positive, negative, and neutral based on expectation, how these are managed, and the level of reality attached to the expectations and perceptions.

  We tend to view negative emotion as a negative thing, but in the service partnership, it can be a positive indication that needs and wants are being managed properly, and for some, the reality of what is achievable and agreed as part of the service agreement is settling in. If there are opportunities for improvement that might have been neglected, this can drive either partner toward a negative emotion because it hasn't been realized, perhaps due to unresponsive management or interaction between the partners. Either situation is a clear indication that active management is needed to stabilize emotions in the relationship.

- Stereotypes—Both the customer and the ITSP will have perceptions of each other, and it's likely that there will be both positive and negative ones. We must accept that this is the case and strive to reduce the negative when possible. Negative stereotypes generally arise from experiences sometimes based upon misconceptions about what should be and not what is—unless, of course, we consistently do not meet our agreed obligations within the partnership, in which case the stereotype might be valid! In Figure 7-1, each has a stereotypical view of the other which could be based in perception or from experience. Understanding what leads to the stereotype is a message with information about how or whether it needs to be changed.

"I am having trouble completing your feedback form. Would you say you are an overachieving under performer, or an underachieving over performer?"

FIGURE 7-1   Example of stereotypes[1]

Like all other quadrants on the compass, stereotypes need to be actively managed to ensure that they are accurate, are based in fact, are not colored by unmanaged needs or wants, and that they serve as a sign that the relationship is healthy, evolving, and maturing over time.

[1] Cartoon adapted with permission of ITEMS LTD., 2011

The balance between the compass points illustrates the perceptions that are created by behaviors and our "experiences" within the partnership. Monitoring these as we do a service-focused balance scorecard is a gauge of how the partnership is working.

Let's look at what various balances and imbalances within the partner compass create within the relationship. Figure 7-2 illustrates the points of balance and imbalance that can occur.

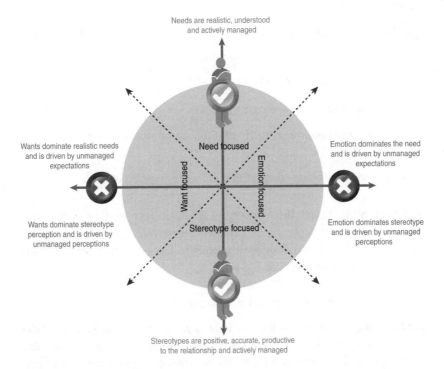

FIGURE 7-2   The partner compass

Within this range, the partnership is in a well-balanced level. Recall that we accept that all compass points will be somewhat dynamic and changing, so the range accounts for this and gives room to identify the triggers that cause a shift to occur and react to them by taking appropriate actions to restore balance.

Symptoms to look for when balance exists:

Services will be operating consistently within the agreed service levels and the customer service experience is fairly predictable, smooth, and expected. Each party is actively engaged in the relationship and managing expectations, making course corrections to keep them in balance, recognizing triggers that affect the balance, and working together to identify the causes and affect the behaviors, changes, and actions that restore the points of balance.

Service outcomes to look for:

- High customer satisfaction ratings
- High business productivity levels
- Balanced performance scorecard
- Little unexpected service disruption, all of which is addressed within targets
- Service-related meetings occurring as regularly planned

Within this range, the partnership is out of balance. One or the other and possibly both partners may experience negative emotions and stereotypes about the other that generally leads to the sense that needs are not being met within the partnership.

Symptoms to look for when an imbalance exists:

Services may be experiencing frequent periods of disruption and service level targets breached. The customers may be stating expectations that conflict with the agreed service levels or terms of the contract. There may be periods of lapsed communication between parties and a sense that either is unreceptive to amicable discussion.

Service outcomes to look for:

- Poor satisfaction ratings
- Frequent service disruptions
- Increased calls to the Service Desk
- Numerous change or service requests that are ambiguous
- Lost business productivity

- Business changes requested as emergency requests

- Service reports that have more excuses than solutions

- Customers contacting IT specialists instead of using agreed channels

- Complaints escalating within the management chains of both customer and ITSP

So, how do you keep the compass in the balanced zone?

Service Monitoring

In order to gauge the range of balance or imbalance, the key is monitoring the health of services. If we think of the compass needle that indicates positional movement, we can establish parameters for monitoring the movement that are tied to triggers. Each parameter will have a threshold, beyond which the need for action arises. In ITSM terms, this equates to service monitoring, which is a crucial part of maintaining balance.

This is a good point to introduce the concepts of proactive and reactive service management activities. Using the partner compass along with service metrics, which we have previously discussed, is a great way to identify activities that can predict and respond to fluctuations in service quality.

 Lingo Lesson—Service monitoring is used by the ITSP to check up on how services are performing. This is often done through a combination of system monitoring tools, report analysis, trending, and setting operational service parameters that allow actions to occur based on feedback received via the monitoring process.

Proactive Service Management

The ITSP will set service performance thresholds that trigger notifications when performance deviates from acceptable norms. From a service perspective, this is a trigger point that may require intervention of some kind. The intervention can be simply to record the event for information, or it can require active intervention to correct something before service disruption occurs. Many of us will jot down grocery items on a shopping list when the supply of the items gets low rather than wait to discover we are out of them when we need them. This is a proactive practice.

As a service example, let's look at an email service. Email requires a number of IT components that function together to deliver the email service. One of these will be servers on which to store the messages for each email account. The ITSP will monitor the performance of the servers and have pre-established thresholds for their capacity. If the system monitoring detects that a threshold is approaching the set capacity limit, an event will be triggered to notify the ITSP of a pending problem with email capacity. The ITSP can take action to increase the capacity, balance the capacity across other servers, or other measures to ensure that the capacity threshold is not exceeded. This is proactive service management. The ITSP anticipates the capacity need, monitors it, and corrects an issue before the customer experiences any service issue. This is entirely invisible to the customer.

In the same way, the partner compass should be proactively managed so that problems are avoided and expectations and perceptions are not negatively affected.

Reactive Service Management

No matter how proactively IT services are managed, unexpected things will happen. In a well-managed service partnership, the causes of unexpected occurrences are often those beyond either partner's ability to predict or control. This is a reality of IT service. The key to properly managing this is having plans established and agreed for what will be done when the unexpected does occur during day-to-day service use and creates service disruptions. All technology has the uncanny ability to malfunction and produce unexpected results that affect services. People can also have the uncanny ability to create unexpected conditions with the same results—service disruption. Service monitoring in a reactive sense can either be from system monitoring that detects a problem that has occurred or a person reporting one.

The ITSP should, through the negotiation of the service agreement, already have established a protocol for dealing with the issues.

Both proactive and reactive service management are needed in the everyday service lifecycle. They each play an important role in keeping the partnership in balance and services delivered as agreed, and the consistent application of each is crucial to a healthy ITSM partnership.

A-ha Moment

The ITSM partnership revolves around seeking balance in the partner-ship compass, anticipating needs in advance, and addressing those that cannot be anticipated.

Keeping balance in the ITSM partnership requires each partner to agree on three things:

1. What can be anticipated and how proactive service management will be used.

2. Expect that not everything can be anticipated and have a reactive service management plan to meet the challenge.

3. Both conditions are normal within the service lifecycle. What counts is how you proactively and reactively manage them.

Identifying Trigger Points

As part of the overall service lifecycle, initial and ongoing planning has occurred through the development of business requirements for the ser-vice, the selection of the ITSP(s), negotiation of the service terms and con-ditions, and the launch of the partnership.

Ongoing planning is an inherent part of the partnership that involves stakeholders from across the customer and supply chain. Good planning practices support sustainable service quality and nurture an accessible, positive relationship foundation between the partners. Business change is a dynamic state and necessary for competitive advantage. IT creates an environment to enable swift, profitable business change, and so it is important that the ITSP be part of the planning cycle.

Proactive Triggers

A great way to ensure the partnership players are involved at key points in the planning cycle is to establish triggers that identify when, who, and what come into play along the timeline.

Some typical triggers are as follows:

- Any activity or initiative that may produce a change to business patterns for use of services. These might involve such things as:
  - Marketing or sales cycles that place increased capacity on communication or transactional type services
  - Service improvement reviews where new or improved ways of working and delivering services are explored
  - Business planning activities, either recurring on a predicted timeline, or those that are ad-hoc and in response to mergers, acquisitions, changes in market position, or new initiatives
  - Regular or ad hoc review that may include the following:
    - Service portfolio management review
    - Fiscal investment review
    - Service performance analysis
    - Partner compass analysis
    - Service review meetings
    - IT service continuity testing
    - ITSM maturity assessment
    - Benchmarking or analysis activities
    - Preparing for shareholder meetings
  - Asset transitions, such as equipment lease expiries or license renewals

Within your organization and your ITSM partnership, you may have a list that resembles the preceding or something different. The important thing is that you HAVE a list. And for each possible trigger that can be predicted (proactive), you identify who needs to be consulted, when this should happen, who is accountable, what needs to be considered, and what outcome is needed.

This information then feeds the service lifecycle over again by creating new or changed business outcome statements, a service strategy, design, transition, operation, and so on. Not every part of the service lifecycle may be required for every trigger, but the use of a stakeholder RACI (responsible, accountable, consulted, informed) matrix can really help identify the details and give clarity to all involved.

RACI Matrix

Table 7-1 illustrates a hypothetical matrix for who plays what role in ensuring the appropriate partners are engaged when certain conditions exist that trigger the need to review service needs. The particulars will change depending on what the trigger is, but as a general rule, the ITSP and the customer should create and maintain a series of matrices to ensure that the right people are involved when service needs may change.

TABLE 7-1   RACI Matrix for Service Needs Review Triggers

Review Trigger	Responsible	Accountable	Consulted	Informed
Service portfolio review	Service owner	ITSP	IT department	Business customer
Service review meeting	Service owner IT department	ITSP	Business customer	IT management Business management
Service performance analysis	Service owner	ITSP	IT department	IT management
Marketing initiatives	ITSP	Business management	IT department Service owner	Business management

Service Roles

Within the ITSM spectrum, there are many roles that for the ITSP are intuitive and necessary to manage IT services. As a business customer, you don't need to understand the details of all of these, but there a few that you should insist on in order to ensure that the partnership is productive, and both you and the ITSP are focused on the correct endgame.

Customer Roles

If we think back to the service lifecycle and the ongoing nature of service management, it's clear that you as a customer play a role in all aspects of the lifecycle. These roles will be played by various people, often at various levels within the company. What you call them is not as important as what they deliver. Let's look at a few.

Business Management

As the primary sponsor of the organization's assets, both fiscal and human, the Business Management role will be involved in strategic decision-making, or decisions that have profound impact on the fiscal and organizational resources of the company. Refer to the previous RACI matrix, and note that this role is kept informed of service changes that result from key initiatives and that may have far-reaching impacts.

Business Management also has a key role to play in setting the cultural tone and example of adopting and accepting new ways of working, which ultimately come into play with new ITSP relationships and ITSM practices. Without senior-level management buy-in, the exercise cannot sustain momentum and becomes more costly, both in money and cultural resistance.

Supplier and Contract Management

This role takes accountability for managing the ITSP relationship directly within the partnership from the business side and is responsible for the outcomes produced. The Supplier Management role will interface with Business Management, Service Owners (see the next section), and department management to ensure that needs are being fulfilled and to keep apprised of potential changes (triggers) that might need to be communicated, discussed, and implemented from the ITSP side.

This role is often also accountable for the contractual relationship with the ITSP and will be a key player in the sourcing, negotiation, and ongoing management of the contract.

Service Owners

This is two roles: one on the supply side and one on the customer side. From the customer side, the Service Owner is accountable for the business service(s) associated to particular business processes. For example, the HR Manager or Director may be the accountable Service Owner for all IT services that support the HR operations. This role is expected to liaise with

Supplier Management to articulate needs, identify potential changes, give feedback to current service quality, and be the resident expert regarding the services within their purview.

Super Users

Every company has resident experts who excel with particular areas of company knowledge. Within an ITSM context, Super Users are invaluable to the success of business outcomes. These are people within the workforce who are hands-on users of services. They often work with the services on a daily basis as part of delivering their role in the company and will have superior knowledge about what works, what doesn't, and what is needed to improve productivity, service quality, and overall business outcomes. Super Users are a critical asset to the ITSP and will often be called upon to provide input to proposed service changes, including design, testing, implementation, training, and daily use. Super Users are the thermometer for service usability and generally possess the greatest knowledge about what works. Every Service Owner should seek out and appoint Super Users within their functional areas.

Change Advisory Board Member

The Change Advisory Board's role is to be accountable for considering the impact to the business and IT of proposed changes to services. The Business should be a member of the CAB in order to confirm business impact, risk, and whether or not a change should be approved. Numerous representatives based on the business unit(s) affected and called upon as needed will fill the business CAB member role. The CAB business member will change with the nature and type of change but should be an expert (perhaps the service owner(s)) and have authority to state a position and make decisions on behalf of the business interests.

ITSP Roles

For the most part, the ITSP will have numerous roles within the service lifecycle, and here we will look at those that you should confirm are there to ensure a good base of coverage within your ITSM partnership.

Customer Manager

Sometimes referred to a Business Relationship Manager, the ITSP should designate an individual or team to this role. This role services as the primary interface for decision-making about the services, the partnership, its growth, and evolution. To the ITSP, this role provides the primary source of information regarding business activities. The accountability of this role is to establish and maintain a constructive relationship between the partners and to identify trends that can influence the type of services or level of services needed by the customer. This role can also be an intermediary role where there appears to be a conflict in the requirements for services between the partners or business units.

Service Portfolio Manager

This role is a pivotal one for the ITSP and the customer. As a senior role in the ITSP organization, the Service Portfolio Management role manages the ITSP services as a group of investments with a view to attracting new customers, retaining customers, and ensuring that the portfolio is profitable, managed responsibly, and builds loyalty within the partnerships. This role takes a holistic organizational view to services and will create service packages and options that can be offered to customers both in a general-use sense and specifically to certain customers.

Service Owner

The Service Owner role is accountable for the delivery of a specific service or set of related services. This role works with the Customer Management role to understand business requirements and translate these into services, measures, and components for the ITSP to deliver. The Service Owner will assist in defining service models using business requirements, business outcome statements, and service requests that can be used to develop, improve, and monitor services.

Process Owner

Many ITSP activities are governed by the processes they use to deliver services to the customer. The Process Owner roles are accountable for ensuring that the ITSM processes are designed appropriately for the delivery of services. These roles, although inwardly focused on ITSP processes, must understand the business services being delivered and how ITSP processes enable this. The Process Owners will be responsible for process design, the policies and standards that govern their use in the ITSP organization, and how the customer interacts with them, ensuring that processes are audited for compliance and reviewing them for improvement opportunities.

Service Level Manager

This role spans between the customer and the ITSP and will often be the one most active on a day-to-day basis between the partners. This role, while being part of the operationally-focused roles, is separated here because of its importance as a direct interface with the business. The Service Level Manager role is accountable for service quality and perform- ance of services in relation to the agreed service levels. The Service Level Manager role will often report directly to the business service owners or management regarding issues of service quality, will be accountable for the service reporting, and will have a solid, positive rapport with the busi- ness and a grounded understanding of the customer's needs and cultures.

Operational Management Roles

During the day-to-day delivery of services, the ITSP will employ a num- ber of roles with specific focus toward cause and effect of service delivery and related issues. These roles will often be associated to an ITSM process that is specifically designed to manage an aspect of the service. We won't go into detail about these; however, it is important that you understand which of these the ITSP uses and how your company and users will inter- face with them in the course of consuming services. Experts agree that the following roles are necessary for a mature ITSM practice:

- Incident Manager—Manages the process and activities associated with service disruptions, service requests, and unexpected service issues.

- Problem Manager—Manages the process and activities associated with known service issues related to major or recurring incidents.

- Change Manager—Manages the process and activities for all service changes, including those requested by the customer and those required for service maintenance.

- Configuration Manager—Manages the process and activities for keeping information on service components, how they are connected to each other, and how they support services. This role is intrinsic in identifying potential impact for making changes.

- **Capacity and Availability Manager**—Manages the process and activities to ensure services have enough capacity to meet fluctuating business demands and that services are not disrupted as a result of capacity issues.

- **Service Desk**—This role is accountable for the day-to-day contact with the customer for service incidents and requests. You may still maintain an internal Service Desk for your users to access support, and the ITSP should offer a single point of contact for your Service Desk and technical resources to contact for service incidents and requests. If the ITSP is the point of contact for your users, its role is to manage service incidents and requests directly. Either way, the ITSP must have a clearly defined role for interfacing with you as the customer for day-to-day service needs.

- **Access Management**—This role may be played by numerous individuals and is accountable for ensuring appropriate access permissions for all users of the service and basic security controls for access to your services.

Figure 7-3 illustrates the organization of the preceding roles throughout the service lifecycle.

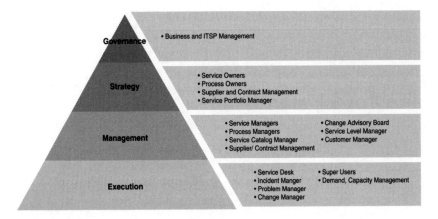

FIGURE 7-3   Service roles within the service lifecycle

A-ha Moment

The ITSM partnership in action revolves around balance—harmony that is kept in check by proactive and reactive actions delegated to specific roles in the partnership. The roles agreed necessary within the partnership will vary with organizational circumstance, but understanding who does what and when in response to a service trigger ensures that the flow of service provision, consumption, and management is mostly predictably managed to the mutual benefit of the partnership.

In the next chapter, we move on to explore what service performance in action looks like and how you ensure that your business benefits from it. We'll also explore how to spot trouble signs and what to do about these.

CHAPTER 8

Service Performance in Action

As we build upon our understanding of IT Service Management, how it supports business success, and some of the key elements you must be in control of within your ITSM partnerships, we now turn our attention to what service performance is all about. Conceivably, a company could have done all the right things when acquiring the services of their ITSP, organized the right roles to support the processes and activities, and still have poor service quality. The way to ensure that you are not one of these statistics is to understand the indicators of good service performance—both of the services themselves and the ITSP who provides them. We now explore how to tell the good from the bad and what to do when you spot trouble.

Service Performance Indicators

In the last chapter, we discussed service monitoring as it related to proactive and reactive actions in a day-to-day service perspective. One of the best ways to keep apprised of how things are going is through the use of performance indicators. ITSM practices use a variety of measures, metrics, and indicators. Here, we explore those most relevant to your business and learn how they apply to service quality, value, and the business bottom line.

Very few companies suffer from lack of data anymore; on the contrary, ITSPs can—and often will—supply you with more data than you could ever read. One of the first things you need to understand is that raw data is of no value to you. It is the ITSP's role to capture, analyze, and present the data in a way that gives you the information to be comfortable about your relationship and perhaps to supply or expand the knowledge you need to make relevant business decisions.

The only reason to explore the raw data would be a lack of trust in the ITSP's reporting of things—and if that is the case, there are more important relationship issues to address than data checking.

Start by asking your ITSP to provide example reports so you get a feel for what they contain and how that is relevant to your business; then decide if they need more, less, or different information. The key question about these reports should be "How does this help me do my job?"

Reports that tell you something you already know or will find out soon anyway are just going to waste your time and cost money you do not need to spend.

Ask yourself three questions as a guide to whether something needs to be measured:

1. How will this information improve my decision-making?

2. Does not knowing this impact my bottom line?

3. Does the value of having this information exceed the cost of getting it?

In all cases, be sure to factor in how long the information on offer will remain valid. If information is volatile, not only will this need to be measured and reported on more often—costing more and taking up more of your time and your staff's time—but you face the chance of believing you know information that you do not, because you trust a report that is out of date.

If you answer *no* to any of these questions, you should reconsider how important the information actually is, and why you would pay to have it collected and reported.

Measuring the Relationship and the Overall Value You Get

Aim to assess, at regular intervals, the quality of the relationship within the ITSM partnership. This covers areas of strength, weakness, vulnerability, and opportunity based on trends that emerge or the level of clarity about strategic indicators of collaborative awareness of the health of IT services.

The CEO of a company needs to know the importance that IT service plays in the delivery of business products and services. As that CEO, what assurances would you need to know about, and how can they be measured? Here are some examples—match the ones you need to the things you care about and the environment your business occupies:

Health warning: Finding things out—through surveys, interviews, and even direct measurement—is a skilled job. If you fully understand representative sampling, placebo effects, self-deception, and skewed reporting, you will probably derive an accurate reflection of what your people think. If not, either get professional skilled help to measure, or beware that your information could be at odds with reality—or even more likely, it is saying something different than you are interpreting:

1. **How satisfied are your employees (and your customers) with the IT services provided?**

   A high level of satisfaction indicates that needs are being met with consistency and are likely well understood and communicated.

   A low level of satisfaction can indicate that needs are not understood and communicated well either by the ITSP or the customer, or that service agreements are not realistic or being reviewed often enough.

   A fluctuating level of satisfaction over short periods of time can indicate inconsistent service practices, or that processes are not working or being consistently followed as they should in either the ITSP or business organization.

   In each case, the information reveals that customer satisfaction can be a barometer to underlying issues that need attention. Left unattended, these can progress into major issues that contribute to a breakdown in partnership trust, negative stereotypes, service disruptions, and lost business productivity. Any of these scenarios will cost you money in some way and are avoidable by simply using KPIs as a window on service quality.

2. **Which of your IT projects support your company's business goals?**

IT projects can take on a life of their own, and not necessarily one that aligns with the original intent. Using KPIs to monitor alignment with business goals can keep them on track and save pain, frustration, and money down the road.

If any projects seem to be moving away from alignment to business objectives, check that business outcome statements are built into the key milestones and that they are being measured regularly. Misalignment creates risk and vulnerability to your business because the outcomes you want might not be what you get, and this will be costlier to fix after the fact.

Service alignment to business objectives should be as much a part of the planning and performance review cycles because there is often a direct cause and effect in cost, alignment, and misalignment. Maintaining that alignment also means reassessing the project if (or, more often, *when*) the business objectives change.

IT projects should be considered within the scope for service management just as live services are. A common problem in companies is a failure to see that, and this can create a situation where misalignment happens because the activities are arm's-length from the service monitoring and review cycles within service management.

3. **How much of your budget goes to ongoing operations versus investments in growth and the business future direction?**

The strongest KPIs in support of this area are those that measure the cost of services in relation to operation and capital investment. There is a tendency to budget only for operational costs, but this can limit the improvement opportunities that would actually save money later on.

An unplanned trend in steadily rising operational costs can indicate that customer "wants" are usurping realistic needs, and the prioritization of service requests based on business need might be out of balance. Aging infrastructure that is not planned for renewal may not be keeping up with the basic service needs and costs more to fix, maintain, and keep operating. This can indicate that strategy and planning or demand management is not being kept aligned with the growth needs of the business.

4. **Do you know the ROI of IT projects before they begin?**

Part of a good service management partnership is ensuring that new services, which typically start as projects, have gone through the design process in such a way as to identify the expected ROI upfront. This provides the basis for strategic decisions about the value of a service or enhancement to a service before the investment is committed.

From a partnership perspective, it helps establish the investment of each party and the returns each should expect. As the service initiative develops, there should be measurements at key milestones in terms of how the investments costs are balancing against any change to the anticipated ROI. This permits corrective action to be taken to bring this into balance and to ensure the outcome will be what each party expects.

5. **What is the cost per day (or per minute) of your most critical services being unavailable?**

Inevitably, there will be times when services experience disruptions of an unplanned nature. The ability of your ITSP to take action to minimize business impact is critical to the health of the relationship. The business must also have contingency measures in place to play its role in returning business to normal when major disruption occurs, so both of these areas of performance are key elements in a positive interaction between partners. Just as important is understanding the cost of disruption to the business. This is a monetary cost as well as indirect impact to business reputation and customer confidence.

Ensuring that performance is measured in terms of cost impact is part of how service performance in general should be managed.

6. **How often does your ITSP not meet your agreed service levels?**

This situation will occur, and any partnership that does not think it can happen is not being realistic. The frequency of this, however, is a direct indicator of potential problems with the service provision.

The reasons can be varied, and KPIs should be closely monitored to determine any trends in this area.

A target is a decreasing rate of missed service levels that result from taking improvement actions after each review. This is a positive indication.

An unchanged rate of missed targets is an unhealthy sign that underlying causes are not addressed, or that the processes that deal with this are not functioning as expected. The root cause might not always be technical in nature. An underfunded ITSP who is forced into best-effort service provision, or continual firefighting just to keep things operating, can never hope to create target improvements without a serious review of funding, resources, or behavioral or strategic changes within the partnership.

It is important to the health of the partnership and to your bottom line that you become adept at understanding the relevant KPIs for performance and that you are as engaged in monitoring and addressing trends and issues as the ITSP is. The partner compass will easily be out of balance, as will the relationship if performance KPIs are not jointly managed.

One of the biggest factors in disrupting the balance are relationships and contractual situations that divide rather than unite the goals of the partners. For example, an ITSP who is paid per Service desk call is not automatically supportive of an organization that needs to reduce calls to the Service desk and is keen to introduce more intuitive systems and empower staff through self-service problem resolution via techniques such as FAQs.

> An increasing rate of missed targets is an indication that the situation is becoming more common, perhaps for the reasons stated in the previous point or something additional has compounded the issue by adding to the underlying cause for poor performance. Again, this is cause for serious concern and action, and rather than look to punitive recourse, a frank discussion to uncover reasons is the best course of action as the starting point.

ITSP Performance KPIs

Having said that you shouldn't overly concern yourself with the internal workings of your ITSP, we do have to interject a bit of reality here. There will be aspects where you need to seek reassurance about the ITSP approach, you will want to see improvements in some of the symptoms that have been upsetting the service value, and you will want to understand enough of the language and mechanism of their work to get a feel for their competence, their performance, and—most of all—their improvement over time.

So, we should consider the more common ways that ITSPs will measure what they do. From the supplier perspective, a process KPI should help to measure the value of how well a process (or service as a whole) was designed and is executed during the provision of service. A KPI generally illustrates the effect on business outcomes to be achieved by measuring effectiveness, efficiency, and performance. In this way, ongoing service performance can be gauged by how well the actual performance stacks up against the KPI.

Here are some examples of service management KPIs.

Incident Management KPIs

The Incident Management process objectives are geared to managing service disruption with minimal impact to the business and restoring services as quickly as possible. From that context, KPIs for this process deal with how process activities have performed toward those objectives. The overarching context is to achieve a high level of service quality and customer satisfaction within the inevitable constraints of cost, resources, time, and so on. Most KPIs will be framed to indicate effectiveness of the incident process, as follows:

- Percentage of incidents resolved without (or negligible) impact to the business

- Percentage of incidents correctly categorized

- Percentage of incidents correctly assigned

- Number of business user complaints regarding incidents

- Average cost per incident

- Total number of incidents

- Percentage of incidents resolved within service level targets

- Percentage of incidents resolved at the first point of contact with the customer

- Percentage of incidents resolved remotely without the need for a customer visit

You might also see—and if you do not, you probably should be seeing—KPIs that aim more to indicate how incidents and the incident management process have affected your business, such as the following:

- Total impact of incidents on the business.

- Performance in dealing with "critical" incidents—ones that stop the business from meeting its objectives.

- Use of resources (and remember that incidents will involve your people as well as the ITSPs, and the costs of both should be measured and considered as the cost of incidents).

Using these types of KPIs, the ITSP will compare these for deviation from the service level targets and the established baseline and develop an opinion of how well the Incident Management process is performing. As each benchmark is taken, the KPIs often have an added criteria of either an increase or decrease in number, percentage, or whatever is relevant to that particular KPI. In that way, performance trends can be evaluated. Some of these KPIs may also be used for development of the service reports.

Change Management KPIs

Change Management is accountable for implementing changes to services. There are two types of change—and from the customer's perspective, you will view them differently:

- Type 1—Changes you want to happen, new things, or different approaches that you have asked for—and are probably paying for. To this end, you are interested in measures that show these changes happened effectively and quickly and delivered the new things you are paying for.

- Type 2—Things the ITSP needs to change—maintenance, technical changes, and so on—from your perspective. You want to see as little evidence of these as possible, so here the rule is to seek demonstration of minimal impact on your business.

KPIs for this process will center on measuring how well the activities have met the following objectives:

- Percentage of changes that met the customer's agreed requirements (this could be broken down into further details, such as cost, quality, time, and so on).

- Average time to implement changes (perhaps broken down by urgency, priority, type of change, service level target, and so on).

- Number of unexpected changes detected—things you did not authorize.

- Percentage of successful changes (and be sure you control what constitutes success).

- Percentage of unsuccessful changes.

- Average cost per change; this should be matched against the value delivered by the change.

Because change inevitably raises the level of risk imposed on the business, the effective performance of this process is of critical business interest in terms of cost, risk, and time to market, so careful attention should be paid in establishing the appropriate KPIs. It is a truism within service management that the biggest negative impact on services is change—especially unauthorized changes—so this is an area from which you might seek evidence if you are having unexpected service issues with your ITSP.

Service Desk KPIs

The Service desk is the direct interface to the business customer for issues, complaints, requests, and assistance. As such, the Service desk is considered the "window of service quality" in the eyes of the customer. From a performance perspective, the Service desk, although technically not a process, is nonetheless an important function within the ITSM partnership to measure the health of at regular intervals. Its effectiveness can be largely attributed to how well the processes used to operate the Service desk are working:

- Number of customer complaints about Service desk communications

- Number of customer requests resolved at first point of contact

- Average wait time for calls to the Service desk

- Average resolution time for incidents and requests

- Number of incidents and requests handled per Service desk agent

- Number of calls abandoned

- Average cost per call

- Number of customer call-backs for information

- Customer satisfaction rating

Most service management experts will agree that poor results for Service desk performance have a directly proportional relationship to the perception of overall service quality. It is critically important that the KPIs established for Service desk performance are realistic, achievable, and unambiguous, and that they can be accurately measured using empirical data and not solely on the basis of perceptions.

Service desk measures need to be interpreted carefully. The Service desk is your staff's everyday route into the ITSP—if it is not an easy route, they will seek alternatives. For many companies, this can mean trying to solve issues themselves—potentially requiring you to pay twice. So, for example, be sure to check behind measures such as falling numbers of calls to the desk—is this happening because fewer things are going wrong or because issues are not being solved when they are reported?

There are almost no limits on what ITSPs can report on these days. The important thing to you as a business customer is considering what is relevant for you to know. As you engage the ITSP in discussions about service agreements, ensure that you make performance measurements a primary topic for agreement. You need to be sure that what you are asking for is achievable and that what you'll get is meaningful.

Remember that although measurements themselves can tell you where you (or your ITSP) are in terms of service quality, looking at how those measurements change over time (finding trends) tells you where you are going—and that is usually much more valuable. So, don't just look at what the measures say now. Instead, see how they have moved over recent reporting periods, compare with how they stood at the same time last year—or better still, map them against your own business cycles.

A-ha Moment

Key Performance Indicators are a barometer for service quality and must be agreed upon as part of the service levels negotiated with the ITSP. They can tell a lot about how well services are performing, and over time, they can often identify the reasons for some service issues.

Partners have a responsibility to understand the value of the KPIs and to participate in the review of them on a regular basis.

Performance Dashboards—A Picture Paints a Thousand Words

After reading the previous points about KPIs, you might be wondering how you can digest all this information in a meaningful way. Many ITSPs offer a visually intuitive means for reviewing service performance information through the use of graphical dashboards. These can be depicted in a variety of ways to help emphasize the importance of key pieces of information to the reader.

The word "dashboard" can be misleading—it sounds like the one master view for controlling things. The modern tools available to ITSPs allow tailored dashboards—that is, they can supply you with an easy interface to see the things you need to see, without swamping them in a sea of other data. If we think back to the KPIs we discussed earlier, we can illustrate the impact of a good and relevant dashboard view in Figure 8-1, which looks at partner and service KPIs combined in various ways to provide different views.

The strength of a dashboard's value is that it represents a condensation of the data being captured specifically targeted to deliver relevant information. The weakness, correspondingly, is that by relying on the dashboard, you might miss an aspect you need to be aware of. So, liaising with your ITSP is still important, as is reviewing its relevance. But overall, seeing a summarized version of what you need allows you to actually take enough time to look and understand—just being faced with the data means most business managers actually look at nothing. So, make sure your ITSP works with you to build what you need.

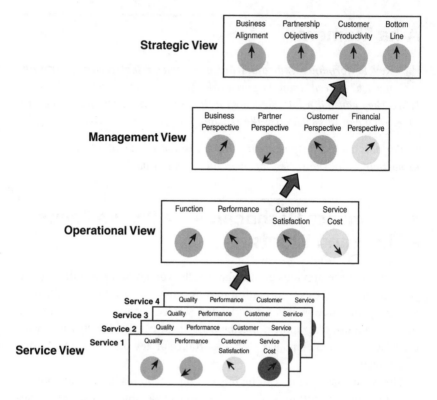

FIGURE 8-1   KPI dashboard view

Figure 8-2 shows the same information, but from differing perspectives.

The dashboard representations should show that copious detail is recorded, and then filtered and assimilated to give each level of management and control the information it needs. It all comes from the same base data—this is important for consistency because it allows one measurement. If you have separate groups measuring separately, you will have no common reference point on which to build discussion and therefore improve upon. For some services, such as those with particular business criticality, or those that are often problematic, drilling down can help draw a more detailed picture. It's the same KPIs being measured, but they are distilled in a different way (see Figure 8-3).

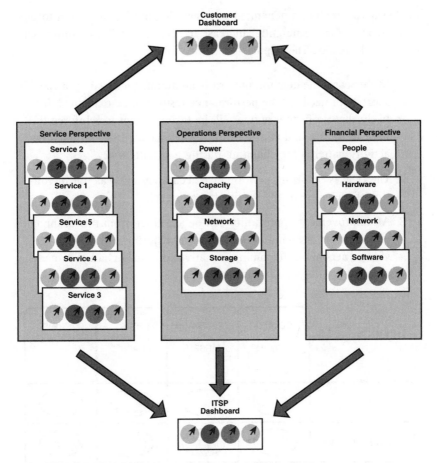

FIGURE 8-2   Dashboard views

This dashboard indicates that demand for three of four services is starting to approach capacity and one (email) has actually exceeded demand during the reporting period. This is a sign that demand forecasts provided during planning are not accurate any longer, and action needs to be taken to understand the reason for this. There may be plausible explanations—for example, a special initiative in the business within sales that has mass

marketed via email and generated sales activity, but has forgotten to prepare the ITSP for the potential increase in service use. These things happen often in reality. The importance is threefold:

1. In this case, the demand pattern is an anomaly caused by a specific
   short-term need, so the performance result can be explained. It is
   likely that no further action will be taken, except to reinforce the
   need to inform and consult with the service owners that business
   activity patterns are changing during a specific time.

2. The ITSP is reporting performance accurately but was not in control of the cause of the service target breach.

3. An improvement opportunity can be identified from this dashboard
   result for better communication from the business units with service owners about upcoming initiatives that may change demand
   patterns.

Service KPI's	DEMAND VS CAPACITY	PERFORMANCE VS TARGETS	SERVICE TARGETS BREACHED	CUSTOMER SATISFACTION
DESKTOP SUPPORT				
SALES APPLICATIONS				
EMAIL SERVICE				
REMOTE ACCESS				

FIGURE 8-3   Performance KPIs by service

The significance of the meaning within the information is that service performance can be patterned, impacts can be seen, and improvement can be
established that create better service quality, better communication, and
better ITSM partnership effectiveness...all from a dashboard!

We can even go a step further in detail if we want to see how the service target breaches happened. Using the preceding example, we know that

email demand exceeded capacity. We also know that this is a corporately shared service. We can predict that once email capacity reaches its limit, users will begin to have problems using the service. They will call the Service desk and the Service desk dashboard KPI, causing two things to stand out:

1. A spike in calls to the Service desk immediately following the capacity issue.

2. An increase in incidents being logged to the email service support teams.

Further dashboard reports on these two areas would reinforce the impact, not only to the business, but increased pressure on ITSP resources that could no longer meet demand. Thus, service targets would be breached.

So, what is the real business lesson here? There are a few:

1. Corporately shared services, such as email, can be dramatically affected by isolated business unit demands. This teaches us that no service is truly independent and that the cause and effect need to be understood across the service.

2. The importance of investing in proactive service management—in this case, capacity monitoring—may have prevented the email service from disruption due to capacity issues.

3. There is always a balance to be achieved for the investment of proactive monitoring and reactive corrective measures. In this particular example, the ROI of monitoring the service may not have been achieved given that this was an anomalous event. The investment in better communication about service demand and link to business initiatives may have accomplished the same result for less investment. There is no absolute here, except that understanding cause and effect can achieve better investment decisions.

4. Further impact was felt by the ITSP who quickly breached service targets during the capacity crisis. This may indicate that resource utilization is high, and there is not much room for meeting service levels during even slight changes in business usage patterns. It could be wise to analyze ITSP resource utilization as a preventative measure for uncertain usage patterns.

All in all, for every rule, there can be exceptions, but using KPIs as an ongoing tool for performance measurement is the best hedge against service performance issues. Pattern analysis, combined with business initiatives and planning with service owners, can uncover gaps in continuity, opportunities for improvement, realignment of resources, and the best chance of meeting service targets sustainably.

A-ha Moment

KPIs are a critical business asset within the ITSM partnership. Having them is not enough—that is just cost. Using them delivers value through service performance trending and usage patterns, and planning for peaks and troughs leads to wise strategic and operational decision-making. This can impact the bottom line favorably with sustained practice. A failure to do this will almost certainly cost you more in the long run.

In the next chapter, we'll bring the poignant messages of this book together and look at how it can improve your business bottom line.

CHAPTER 9

The Bottom Line

At the beginning of this book, I referred to ITSM as documented common sense. After reading the previous eight chapters, I hope you agree that most of what is written in these pages is just that. ITSM is not a magic bullet, and adopting it within your service strategy is just the first step in a journey. The journey is what ITSM is all about—not the destination.

Common Cents

ITSM practices are not unique to IT. If you strip away the IT part, you are left with good common sense about service management in general. Highly successful companies use those things every day. Look at Figure 9-1 and see the similarities to how the lifecycle of service management that began this book aligns to that of any product or service your company might provide to your customers.

Forget about IT service for a moment. Think about your own business. You strive to achieve superior quality in your products and services, and you demand competent suppliers to provide you with the elements you use to create value for your customer. You endeavor to differentiate your company from all others like it, so that your customers remain loyal and new customers keep joining the ranks. You balance the cost of providing products with quality, demand, and profitability. You never stop looking for the next innovation, the next improvement, and the next customer.

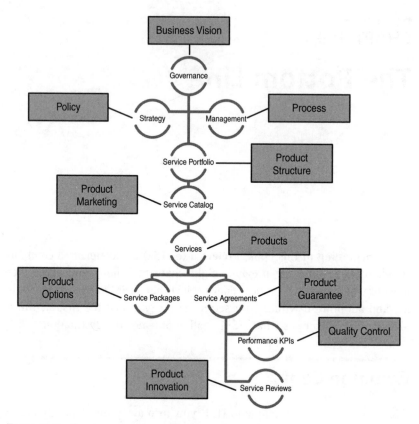

FIGURE 9-1   Service management/business management

ITSM has all the same characteristics. The only difference is that this time YOU are the customer. The best advice any industry expert can give you is to use what you know. Use what you are good at and apply those qualities to your approach to service management.

Above all else, trust your instincts. Something that seems too good to be true usually is. Cheap is not sustainable, and expensive isn't necessary; balance is the key.

Short-changing your ITSPs by trying to squeeze the budget too tight will cost you in quality, reliability, and lasting partnerships. Being too generous just eats away your bottom line. Balance is the key.

Over decades of practice, ITSM has forged ahead and has become a partner to business success. Over decades, the priorities and outcomes for adopting ITSM haven't changed:

- Enabling greater business profitability
- Maintaining peak workforce productivity
- Doing more for less
- Retaining and attracting customers
- Controlling IT costs
- Improving IT service quality
- Aligning IT to business
- Leveraging technology innovations for business success
- Using industry best practices to achieve high-performance IT services and business gains
- Minimizing risk, avoiding failures, and controlling outcomes
- Predicting, planning, and growing the business bottom line

The best place to start your ITSM journey is to look inward. Understand what services mean to you. Understand what you need and what outcomes you are expecting. Test how realistic they are and question everything at least once. The biggest failure in service management relationships is unrealistic expectations bounded by unreasonable demands.

Transformations

Over the years, some poignant business transformations have occurred when committed businesses meet ITSM excellence:

> *"Our company was always a solid performer, but as IT costs began to rise, we just didn't have the resources left over to fund new product innovations. When we adopted ITSM, we saw immediate benefits to our bottom line within the first month. That trend has continued over the past 10 years we've been on the ITSM journey to service excellence. Our customers are happier, our products get to market faster, we beat our competition more often, and we've spent less doing it. We believe that our investment in ITSM has been the reason we've survived economic turmoil and kept on growing through tough times."*
> —CEO, financial industry

"While evaluating potential IT service providers, one proposal in particular caught the attention of our Senior Management. It was the one that predicted we could lower our IT costs by 45 percent within 12 months. There isn't much in the way of investment opportunities that pay those dividends! We were worried that this was nothing more than marketing hype, but on close examination of where the savings would be seen, it became clear that we had no idea of what our services had been costing us. We took what we thought was a cautious approach and started out with this [ITSP] in small incremental adaptation of ITSM. This was made easy for us since this ITSP was already a mature ITSM organization. The results were so significant that we accelerated the adoption, and we did in fact achieve almost 40% savings in the first year. Were we 5% short because we moved more cautiously until we were convinced? NO, we were 40% ahead. Ask me if I'm a believer in ITSM!"
—IT Director, pharmaceutical industry

A major credit card company engaged an IT provider who used ITSM to help manage critical business systems and software distribution to its numerous global office locations. System downtime was costing the company millions each month in lost business. Their use of ITSM resulted in a 30% reduction in service outages, and within 24 months, a 92% reduction in critical incidents. In addition, the company reduced its IT support costs by 20%. These savings covered the transition and implementation costs in the first two years.

A large health and beauty product manufacturer started its ITSM journey by targeting a 6% savings in operational costs as its objective. Its journey, now over 10 years old, continues to create increased profitability by about $125 million dollars annually.

You wouldn't consider starting a company without a plan. You wouldn't create a business plan without understanding your market and its customers. You wouldn't make promises to business partners or customers that you couldn't keep. Business success hinges on the right ideas, at the right time, in the right market, and some lucky breaks along the way. Creating the right things at the right time takes forethought, planning, governance, strategy, design, transition, operation, and continual improvement. That cycle never stops moving, and changes in innovation, economic climate, appetite for risk, and the next right idea at the right time is always just around the corner. ITSM can help create the next right idea at the right time, but its ability to deliver on promises requires all these same ingredients, from planning to continual innovation and improvement.

Your Bottom Line

The preceding examples are but a few of the many in the ITSM industry that boast success stories. Every year, more examples join the ranks of businesses that have harnessed the power of ITSM by using it within their ITSP partnerships.

This book brings together the key concepts of IT Service Management with the experience of decades of ITSM partnerships. The mainstay of every business and IT partnership is the knowledge that ITSM requires a holistic approach from governance to operation and is an ongoing journey where a balanced view of the health of the partnership, the services, and the practices enable them to flourish. Even the best ideas at the right time can be made better with solid service management behind them.

The concepts presented in this book are real. They are adapted from the best practices in the service management industry. They are used every day around the world in every type of industry.

The guidance in this book is supported by the world's foremost thought leaders in business and ITSM and has been formulated from my 30 years as an expert in this field.

ITSM has been proven beyond doubt to deliver on its promises, but it isn't something you *do*. It's something you *create* with common sense, intuitive business sense, and a commitment to never stop looking for ways to improve. ITSM is a journey for everyone who wants his or her company to unlock its full potential and improve its bottom line.

That sounds an awful lot like good business sense to me!

APPENDIX A

IT Strategy Template

This template sets out a suggested format for an IT strategy document, together with a checklist for the content of the strategy itself.

Individual strategy documents may vary to take account of particular requirements or planning situations. The checklist may still provide planning groups with a useful tool to ensure that their strategy is able to be read consistently with others developed within the organization, and that it provides a basis for evaluation, review, and improvement.

Key points to consider:

1. Use plain English, and avoid jargon wherever possible. Where it is unavoidable, give the full meaning of any abbreviations the first time they are used and include a glossary with the meanings of any technical terms and/or abbreviations at the end of the document.

2. Other supporting material (such as sections of policy documents and so forth) can be appended, but unless they need to be referred to frequently by everyone using the document, it may be better to include a reference to them rather than the actual material.

3. Include a list of references at the end, including any other document that has been mentioned in the text.

4. Keep in mind that a strategy document is not an end within itself. The strategy is a vision for improving services, and it is how it is translated into action that is the real measure of its success.

ABC Corporation
IT Strategy

Document Control Information	
Document Details	
Document Name	
Purpose of Document	
Document Version Number	
Document Status	
Document Owner	
Prepared By	
Date Approved	
Approved By	
Master Service Contract Ref	
Core Service Agreement Ref (If Applicable)	
Next Scheduled Review Date	

Version History

Version Number	Date Approved	Reasons for Version Change

Document Distribution

Version	Name	Organization/Role

Section	Content	Checklist
Introduction	Status of this document	• Is this a draft strategy for consultation or a finished version?
	The scope of the strategy	• What does this strategy cover (IT services, IT service portfolio, and so on)? This is referred to as ABC in the sections below. What does it not cover (for example, children or older people)?
	The overall aim of the strategy	• An outline of what you are trying to achieve (for example, solving a problem with ABC, improving ABC services, introducing services to a new area, reorganizing services, and so on).
	The timescale of the strategy	• What is the target date for achieving this strategy?
	Constraints on this strategy	• Does this strategy need to be coordinated with others outside ABC (for example, ITSPs or business units/partners)?
	The development process	• Who is leading on the development of this strategy (for example, director/lead/manager)? • Who else is involved? • What work has taken place to date on the development of the strategy? • Specifically, how have service users, owners, providers, and other staff been consulted and involved?
Stakeholder analysis	Analysis of who the stakeholders are, and their needs/expectations in relation to the strategy	• Who are the stakeholders in ABC (internal and external groups)? • To what extent are all these stakeholders currently engaged? • What evidence do we have for how ABC is perceived by each group of stakeholders, and what are their needs/expectations/priorities? • How will we tackle gaps in the existing information we have about stakeholders as part of this strategy?

Section	Content	Checklist
Strategic vision and values	A statement of the vision for ABC in the future	• What, in overall terms, will success look like? (This can be a qualitative description of the long-term vision for ABC—the quantitative data that will help assess how far this has been achieved in three years will be set out in sections below.)
	The values that are central to this strategy	• What are the core values on which this strategy is based, and which will inform all the actions that are planned as a result?
The current position **(Where are we now?)**	Purpose and objectives	• What is the purpose of ABC/why does it exist at all? • What are the objectives of ABC?
	Policy context	• What current policy affects ABC? What does it say? (This may include both directly relevant policy—for example, an NSF or other NHS/social care policy, and policy in other areas with an impact on ABC, such as housing, education, employment, benefits, and so on.)
	Current dimensions	• How many current users/clients are there for ABC? What are the significant markets within the overall user base? Is there an assessment of unmet demand? • What services are currently provided in ABC and by whom? What financial data is there on ABC (such as total spent, breakdown by localities, recent investment levels, or sources of external funding)?
	Current performance	• What evidence is there of the outcomes achieved in ABC at present? (Note: This should link to the key performance results identified below, where possible.) • Are trends over time positive or negative? • How does the ABC compare with other organizations now? • What changes are already in progress in ABC, and how might they affect the key performance results (for example, a new service development coming on stream in year 1 of the strategy)?

Section	Content	Checklist
	Workforce analysis	• How many people are involved in delivering ABC? How is this overall number made up (for example, by locality, profession, provider, and so on)?
		• What is the current position on vacancies/turnover/training places, and so on?
		• What training is currently provided and to whom? Does this include all relevant providers (for example, voluntary/independent sector)?
	Information analysis	• What sources of information on ABC are used currently?
		• How are new ideas and learning about ABC gathered, analyzed, and used?
	Process analysis	• What are the key processes through which ABC is delivered?
		• Do we know how these processes work and therefore how changes in one part of the process can result in a change in the results achieved?
Strategic objectives	Where do we want the organization to be in three years' time?	• What are the key performance results we want to have achieved in three years' time, based on what we know about stakeholders' needs and expectations, which will demonstrate that we have moved toward achieving the vision for ABC?
		• What are the relevant operational indicators (internal measures that have an effect on outcomes)? For example, if one key performance result is the waiting time for service restoral, how many staff currently perform this service and what are the vacancy/staff turnover rates for them?
	Evidence that achieving these strategic objectives will contribute to the overall objectives of ABC as expressed in its mission, vision, and values.	• How will the ABC compare with other organizations?
		• Do we need to collect different information/information in a different form to enable us to measure the key performance results?
		• How will these results contribute to the overall performance of the ABC?

Section	Content	Checklist
Priorities for strategic change	The main areas where change is needed to enable us to achieve our strategic objectives	• What gaps have been identified in the current situations that need to be filled (including stakeholder involvement, information, and so on)?
		• What options have been considered for strategic change and on what basis have the decisions been made on which to progress?
		Strategic change will involve changes to the existing key processes identified previously (and if these are not well understood, the starting point will be work to identify and define them), or developing new processes to deliver a specific outcome.
		Process change should aim to deliver agreed, improved outcomes and should involve all relevant stakeholders (both internal and external).
		Changing existing key processes or developing new ones may involve changes in any or all of:
		• The **workforce** (for example, staffing numbers and/or roles, training, or communications).
		• The **partnerships** ABC has with other organizations.
		• How **resources** are used.
		• The **funding** available and/or how this is deployed.
		• Corporate **policy** and/or other strategies that affect ABC.
		• What is the timescale for each of the changes above (that is, in which year of the strategy will work take place)?
		• Who will lead on each change area?
		• How do we expect the key performance outcomes and operational indicators to change each year as changes are made?

Section	Content	Checklist

Workforce issues	The impact of the strategic changes on the ABC workforce	• Section 6 should include workforce implications of each change—this section brings these individual changes together.
		
		• What will be the overall impact of the strategy on workforce:
		
		  • What skills are required and how can these be provided (which professionals can best provide these)?
		
		  • What training/skills development is needed to achieve the strategy, and how will this be addressed?

Evaluation, learning, and review	How progress will be measured, and the strategic objectives reviewed, with stakeholders' involvement	• Plan for how stakeholder groups will be involved in ongoing evaluation and review of the strategy throughout its life. • Arrangements for measuring performance over the lifetime of the strategy, and reviewing the strategic objectives. • Arrangements for developing action plans to maintain progress against the key performance results and/or take corrective action where performance is below expected levels. • Arrangements for gathering and using innovation and learning (internal and external) to inform the strategy.
Communication plan	How this strategy will be communicated to all stakeholders	• Plan for communicating the content of the strategy, and ongoing progress, to all stakeholder groups (taking into account differing needs/expectations/levels of involvement).
Contact information		• Who is the contact person for queries/suggestions/comments? • Is there a deadline for comments on this document (for example, if it is a draft for consultation)?

Section	Content	Checklist
Glossary		
References		
Year 1 action plan	Action to be taken in year 1 toward the achievement of the strategic objectives	• Detailed plans for actions to be implemented in year 1 to achieve the planned changes in key performance results/operational indicators. • This should show the following for each action point: 　• The resource implications (staffing, information, physical resources, service assets, and finance). 　• Who is responsible for delivering each action point. 　• When it will be completed. 　• Which key performance result(s) it is targeted at.
Year 2/3 action plans	Future years' action plans will be developed as a result of the following: • Analyzing key performance results and operational indicators, and setting appropriate targets for these in the year to come. • Assessing changes in the external environment affecting ABC (for example, new national targets, or changes in other health and social care organizations). • Analyzing innovation and learning relevant to ABC. • Reviewing how this strategy fits with the overall corporate direction.	

APPENDIX B

Service Contract Template

The Service Contract template covers the basic information an organization should include. Ensure that you have adapted this template to your organization's needs and have vetted it with legal, corporate policy and standards areas for compliance.

Because many states, regions, countries have differing legal requirements; it's a good practice to consider this as a starting point from which to build.

Service Contract

This contract made

BETWEEN
ABC COMPANY
("CORPORATION")
-AND-
XYZ IT SERVICE PROVIDER
("ITSP")

As the Corporation has the authority to enter into this binding agreement with the ITSP for the provision of IT services;

AND AS the Service Provider has agreed to provide services described in the pursuant core and service agreements;

THEREFORE THE PARTIES agree as follows:

Definitions

1. In this contract,

    a. Corporation means...

    b. Staff means...

    c. Service provider means...

    d. Customer means...

    e. Service means...

    f. (All pertinent definitions should be included.)

Services

2. The Service Provider agrees to provide the "services" in accordance with the policies, guidelines, and requirements of the Corporation.

3. The Corporation agrees to fulfill its responsibilities under the contract and pursuant agreements in support of the fulfillment of the services by the Service Provider.

Term

4. This contract will be in force from (date), unless superseded by a subsequent contract, or either party terminates it in its entirety by giving (day) written notice. In the event of a termination, the Corporation will pay any monies due for the services rendered prior to the date of termination and likewise, the Service Provider will refund any monies for services not provided but having been paid for by the Corporation prior to the date of termination.

Consideration

5.

   a. The Corporation will pay to the Service Provider, for admissible expenditures related to the provision of the "services" and amount not to exceed that stipulated hereto.

   b. The parties agree that while this agreement is in force, the approved budget will be negotiated on or before the start of the applicable fiscal year while this contract is in force.

   c. The Service Provider may elect to transfer funds within the total budget for the provision of services as needed without prior approval, but no funds may be transferred outside of the overall budget specifically approved for the provision of the "services."

   d. It is agreed that the Corporation may withhold payment if the Service Provider is in breach of the pursuant service agreements. *(You can be more specific here about what, how much, and under what conditions penalties will be applied.)*

   e. The Corporation will permit access to the authorized staff of the Service provider to the Corporation's premises for the purpose of providing the "services." The Corporation reserves the right to screen and authorize access to the Service Provider in the manner appropriate to the security policies of the Corporation.

   f. The corporation and the service provider will ensure the fulfillment of roles and responsibilities as agreed and documented for each service agreement under this contract.

Reports

6.

   a. The Service Provider will maintain service records respecting each site where service is being provided and prepare and submit at such intervals as indicated in the attached Schedule(s), a report respecting the Services being provided pursuant to this contract, acceptable to the Corporation which shall include service information such as statistics on target achievements, and such other information as the Corporation requires. The report's details will be specifically defined in the service agreements.

b. The Service Provider will also prepare and submit to the Corporation, quarterly, or at any time upon reasonable request, a comprehensive report acceptable to the Corporation respecting the performance overall of all services being provided under this contract.

Financial Records and Reports

7.

a. The Service Provider will maintain financial records and books of account respecting services provided pursuant to this contract for each site where service is being provided and will allow the Corporation or such other persons appointed by the Corporation to inspect and audit such books and records at all reasonable times both during the term of this contract and subsequent to its expiration or termination.

b. The Service Provider will, unless the Corporation indicates otherwise, submit to the Corporation within thirty (30) days of the calendar year end:

i. A Financial Statement with respect to

1. The services provided pursuant to this agreement.

2. An audited Financial Statement with respect to the services provided pursuant to this agreement.

c. The Service Provider will retain the records and books of account referred to in clause 7(a) for a period of seven (7) years.

8. Provider's financial year end as a detailed operational financial report in such form and containing such information as the Corporation may require.

Confidentiality

9. The Service Provider, its directors, officer, employees, agents, and volunteers will hold confidential and will not disclose or release to any person other than approved Corporation staff at any time during or following the term of this contract, except where required or permitted by law, any

information or document that tends to identify any individual in receipt of services without obtaining the written consent of the Corporation.

Indemnification

10. The Service Provider will, both during and following the term of this contract, indemnify and save harmless the Corporation from all costs, losses, damages, judgments, claims, demands, suits, actions, complaints, or other proceedings in any manner based upon, occasioned by or attributable to anything done or omitted to be done by the Service Provider, its directors, officer, employees, agents, and volunteers in connection with services provided, purported to be provided or required to be provided by the Service Provider pursuant to this contract.

Insurance

11. The Service Provider will obtain and maintain in full force and effect during the term of the contract, general liability insurance acceptable to the Corporation in an amount of not less than $XXXXX.XX dollars per occurrence in respect of the services provided to this contract.

   a. The insurance policy shall

      i.   include as an additional insured A the Corporation in respect of and during the provision of services by the Service Provider pursuant to this contract;

      ii. contain a cross-liability clause endorsement; and

      iii. contain a clause including liability arising out of the contract or agreement.

   b. The Service Provider will submit to the Corporation, upon request, proof of insurance.

Termination

12. Either party may terminate this contract in whole or in part with respect to the provision of any particular services upon (XX)-day notice to the other party. If the contract is terminated in part, all obligations with respect to the provision of all other services continue in full force and effect.

Freedom of Information

13. Any information collected by the Corporation pursuant to this contract is subject to the rights and safeguards provided for in the Freedom of Information and Protection of Privacy Act *(or applicable act)*.

Disposition of Assets

14. The Service Provider will not sell, change the use, or otherwise dispose of any items, furnishings, or equipment purchased with the Corporation's funds pursuant to this contract without the prior written consent of the Corporation, which may be given subject to such condition as the Corporation deems advisable.

Amendments

15. This contract may be amended by substitution of the Schedules, duly signed by the parties to this contract.

Non-Assignment

16. The Service Provider will not assign this contract, or any part thereof, without the prior written approval of the Corporation, which approval may be withheld by the Corporation in its sole discretion or given subject to such conditions as the Corporation may impose.

Schedules

17. All the terms of the Schedules are incorporated into this contract except where they are inconsistent with this contract. This contract and the attached Schedules embody the entire contract and supersede any other understanding or contract, collateral, oral or otherwise, existing between the parties at the date of execution and relating to the subject matter of this contract.

Laws

18. The Service Provider agrees that the Service Provider and its employees and representatives, if any, shall at all times comply with any and all applicable federal, state, and municipal laws, ordinances, statues, rules, regulations, and orders in respect of the performance of this contract.

IN WITNESS WHEREOF this contract has been signed by an authorized corporate official on behalf of the Corporation and the Service Provider by its proper signing officers.

Signed, sealed, and delivered

On the day of , _____20XX.

_____   _____

On behalf of the Corporation   On behalf of the Corporation

_____   _____

On behalf of the Service Provider

Service Agreement Template

Document Control Information		
Document Details		
Document Name		
Purpose of Document		
Document Version Number		
Document Status		
Document Owner		
Prepared By		
Date Approved		
Approved By		
Master Service Contract Ref		
Core Service Agreement Ref (If Applicable)		
Next Scheduled Review Date		

Version History		
Version Number	**Date Approved**	**Reasons for Version Change**

Document Distribution

Version	Name	Organization/Role

General Information

This is a service agreement between ABC company and XYZ service provider. The intent of this agreement is to document the following:

- The details of 123 core service (a particular core service or service package).
- The terms and conditions of how the service is managed.
- The responsibilities of each party in the execution of this agreement.

Agreement Term

The date the agreement is in effect.

Definitions

The following terms are used throughout this service agreement. The definitions included here are intended to clarify the meaning of these terms relevant to how they are used in this agreement.

Term	Definition

Service Description

A brief, business-focused description of what the service is. As an example, an email service could be described as follows: This service allows

XYZ employees to receive, send, and store electronic messages from their corporately authorized desktop computers and mobile devices.

Include a brief outline of the basic business functionality of the service.

Include a list of assumptions that the provision of the service takes into account. Some examples are as follows:

- Upgrades to this service will be handled as projects outside the scope of this agreement.

- Service will be provided in adherence to corporate and legislated policies and procedures.

- Changes to services will be documented and communicated to all stakeholder on the change schedule posted on the corporate change intranet {URL}.

Hours of Coverage

The hours of availability of the service to its customers. Example: Monday to Friday 9:00 am–5:00 pm local time, or 24 hours a day, 7 days per week, excluding regularly scheduled maintenance Sundays at 5:30 am GMT.

Be clear on what local time means, and if there are multiple time zones covered, list these specifically to aid in clarity.

Roles and Responsibilities

List all relevant roles for the service and include the ITSP and the business. Start with the primary stakeholders. An example is:

Stakeholder	Title/Role	Contact Information
Service Owner	Business reps	
Service Owner	ITSP rep	
Customer support	ITSP service desk	
Change Manager	ITSP rep	
Change Advisory Board Chair	ITSP rep	

Stakeholder	Title/Role	Contact Information
Service inquiries	ITSP service desk	
Service requests	ITSP service desk	
Complaints	ITSP service desk	
Communication	Business/ITSP reps	

ITSP Responsibilities

This is a brief outline of what the ITSP is expected to be responsible for under the terms of the agreement. These are basic, concise statements that frame how the ITSP will be judged to be in compliance with the agreement. Examples:

- Meet response times associated with this agreement for issues, complaints, requests, and so on.

- Generate service reports on time in accordance with the agreed schedule and reporting format.

- Provide agreed advance notice of scheduled maintenance via (name the communication methods).

- Include the details and options of this service in the Service Catalog.

- Ensure availability of reps as indicated to respond and participate in the execution of their roles under this agreement.

- Adhere to all corporate, legislative, and operational standards and policies as agreed.

- Endeavor at all times to uphold the spirit, intent, and harmonious partnership that this agreement implies.

Customer responsibilities:

- Ensure availability of reps as indicated to respond and participate in the execution of their roles under this agreement.

- Adhere to all corporate, legislative, and operational standards and policies as agreed.

- Endeavor at all times to uphold the spirit, intent, and harmonious partnership that this agreement implies.

- Communicate business outcomes and requirements regarding the operation and improvement or changes to this service.

Service Support

Service Requests

A brief definition of what a service request is agreed to be, along with details of how the customer makes the request.
Example:
A service request for this service includes the following:

- Move an email account to a different business unit.

- Add user accounts to any business unit.

- Change user account information or password.

- Request additional email storage space temporarily or permanently.

- Service enhancements or changes to functionality.

All service requests must be made to the XYZ Service Desk using one of the following approved methods:

- Logging a service request ticket on the Self-Service portal (URL).

- Contacting the Service Desk during operating hours via telephone, fax, or email (provide details).

Service Disruption

Any incident that causes an unexpected or unplanned service disruption or should be reported as soon as possible by contacting the XYZ Service Desk.

Response

The following service response targets are agreed:

Type of Incident	Agreed Business Impact	Response Target	Resolve Target
Single user affected	Non-critical	2 hour	4 hours
Multiple users within a single business unit affected	Non-critical	1 hour	2 hours
Multiple business units affected	Non-critical	.5 hour	1 hour
Single user affected	Critical	15 minutes	30 minutes
Multiple users within a single business unit affected	Critical	10 minutes	20 minutes
Multiple business units affected	Critical	5 minutes	10 minutes

These are arbitrary targets but indicate a scale of impact urgency and priority.

NOTE: Often, ITSPs will include a lot of throughput, volume, and percentage availability information in a service agreement. UNLESS this is understood and considered critical to the business to see this reported, it is likely not relevant to the understanding of performance. For example, is it as important for you to know the service availability is 99.9% each month, or that it experiences X disruption of Y duration? Be clear about how you want to see service performance stated in the agreement and reported on.

Escalation

If the XYZ Service Desk is unable to directly resolve the incident, the following escalation protocols are agreed.

Document these similar to the preceding table with target times and service tiers/management.

Exceptions to Service Coverage

If services or support will be unavailable for any duration such as statutory holidays or other special exception, these should be listed here.

Other Requests

Use this area to define access and type of additional requests, such as special reporting, support extensions for special business circumstances, and so on. Be sure to include information on who is authorized to make special requests, who must approve them, and how they will be handled.

Service Maintenance and Changes

Include the regular service maintenance windows that stipulate when the service will not be available for use by the business and how changes that are not included as part of regular occurring maintenance will be communicated and implemented.

Service Costs

Here, the relevant cost, pricing, and charging information must be included. It's a good idea to review the headings and identify costs this way, if that is appropriate, such as per business unit per month, per incident, per change, and so on. This may be too detailed; in that case, stick with a simpler service per month cost, BUT under all conditions be sure to articulate these clearly and accurately.

Service Reporting

Include the reporting frequency, and refer to an appendix or example of the service report, who reviews it, when it is due, and who owns the responsibility for maintaining the service reports.

Audits

You may want to include information about when, who, and what will be audited about the service. Often this is done at the service contract level, in which case, unless there are specific service-related audit requirements, you may want to include them in the contract.

Document Location

Be sure to indicate where the service agreement is kept, how it is accessed, and by whom.

Appendices

Any relevant supporting documentation, schedules, processes, and so on can be included as appendices to the agreement.

To determine if this is necessary, ask yourself if you are willing to put in place the processes to ensure that these appendices are kept updated when the original documents are changed or updated in any way. If this isn't done, the appendices are not worth including because out-of-date information is as bad as no information. Electronic links are often a way to ensure synchronous version control.

APPENDIX D

References for Further Reading

The topic of IT Service Management is fairly broad, and there are many publications, white papers, blogs, and feeds related to the practice of ITSM. A good deal of published ITSM information is sponsored by commercial vendors who share thought leadership, and others by trade associations who share ideas, experiences, and adapted best-practice use.

The following list is a compilation of further reference from official best-practice framework libraries, trade association publications, and web-sites that offer insight, experiences, and information.

The following references are those specifically discussed within this book and/or authored, co-authored, or architected by Sharon Taylor:

ITIL V2: The Business Perspective (Contributing Author); 2006, Office of Government Commerce, Publisher; TSO, The Stationary Office.
ISBN: 9780113308941

ITIL V2—Small-Scale Implementations (Co-Author); 2006, Office of Government Commerce, Publisher; TSO, The Stationary Office.
ISBN: 9780113309801

ITIL V3—ITIL Service Management Practices; ITIL Service Strategy (Chief Architect); 2007, Office of Government Commerce, Publisher; TSO, The Stationary Office.
ISBN: 9780113310456

ITIL V3—ITIL Service Management Practices; ITIL Service Design (Chief Architect); 2007, Office of Government Commerce, Publisher; TSO, The Stationary Office.

ISBN: 9780113310470

ITIL V3—ITIL Service Management Practices; ITIL Service Transition (Chief Architect); 2007, Office of Government Commerce, Publisher; TSO, The Stationary Office.

ISBN: 9780113310487

ITIL V3—ITIL Service Management Practices; ITIL Service Operation (Chief Architect); 2007, Office of Government Commerce, Publisher; TSO, The Stationary Office.

ISBN: 9780113310463

ITIL V3—ITIL Service Management Practices; ITIL Continual Service Improvement (Chief Architect); 2007, Office of Government Commerce, Publisher; TSO, The Stationary Office.

ISBN: 9780113310494

ITIL V3—The Official Introduction to the ITIL Service Lifecycle (Author); 2007, Office of Government Commerce, Publisher; TSO, The Stationary Office.

ISBN: 978011331061

ITIL V3—Key Element Guides for Service Strategy, Design, Transition, Operation, Improvement (Chief Architect); 2007, Office of Government Commerce, Publisher; TSO, The Stationary Office.

ISBN: 97801133119, 20, 21, 22

ITIL V3—Passing Your Foundation Exam; *The Official Study Aid*, First Edition (Chief Architect); 2007, Office of Government Commerce, Publisher; TSO, The Stationary Office.

ISBN: 9780113310791

ITIL V3—Small-Scale Implementation (Co-Author); 2007, Office of Government Commerce, Publisher; TSO, The Stationary Office.

ISBN: 9780113310784

Creating and Sustaining Service Excellence: The Executive's Guide to Service Management; Due out August 2011; itSMF International: 2011, TSO, The Stationary Office ISBN: 9780117069022.

http://www.itsmfi.org/content/publications

The following section contains further reading references for ITSM-related practices discussed in this book and authored by third parties:

IT Service Management Forum Publications

http://www.itsmfi.org/content/publications

The eSourcing Capability Model for Client Organizations (eSCM-CL) v1.1

William Hefley and Ethel Loesche

http://www.itsqc.org/downloads/documents/eSCM-CL_Part1_V1dot1.html

COBIT Framework for Governance and Control; VAL IT, RISKIT

IT Governance Institute; Information Systems Audit and Control Association

http://www.isaca.org/Knowledge-Center/Pages/default.aspx

ISO/ IEC Standards for ITSM: 20000, 27000, 38500, 9001

http://www.iso.org/iso/home.htm

Capability Maturity Model Integration

http://www.sei.cmu.edu/cmmi

Additional thought leadership white papers, articles, blogs, and podcasts featuring the author of *Service Intelligence* can be found at the following website:

www.aspect360.net

Index

J-K

L

M

S

FREE Online Edition

Your purchase of **Service Intelligence** includes access to a free online edition for 45 days through the Safari Books Online subscription service. Nearly every Prentice Hall book is available online through Safari Books Online, along with more than 5,000 other technical books and videos from publishers such as Addison-Wesley Professional, Cisco Press, Exam Cram, IBM Press, O'Reilly, Que, and Sams.

SAFARI BOOKS ONLINE allows you to search for a specific answer, cut and paste code, download chapters, and stay current with emerging technologies.

Activate your FREE Online Edition at
www.informit.com/safarifree

> **STEP 1:** Enter the coupon code: TZPPYYG.

> **STEP 2:** New Safari users, complete the brief registration form.
> Safari subscribers, just log in.

If you have difficulty registering on Safari or accessing the online edition, please e-mail customer-service@safaribooksonline.com